FILIP BONDY

WHO'S ON WORST?

Filip Bondy is a sports columnist for the New York *Daily News*. He has been cited as one of the top ten sports columnists in America by the Associated Press Sports Editors. His articles have appeared in *The New York Times*, *Sports Illustrated*, *GQ*, and *The Village Voice*. He has also authored or coauthored six books, including *Tip-Off* and *Chasing the Game*.

Also by Filip Bondy

WHO'S ON WORST?

FILIP BONDY | WHO'S ON WORST?

The Lousiest Players, Biggest Cheaters,
Saddest Goats and Other Antiheroes
in Baseball History

ANCHOR SPORTS

Anchor Books
A Division of Random House LLC
New York

FIRST ANCHOR SPORTS EDITION, FEBRUARY 2014

The Library of Congress has cataloged the Doubleday edition as follows:
Bondy, Filip
Who's on worst? : the lousiest players, biggest cheaters, saddest
goats and other antiheroes in baseball history / Filip Bondy.
p. cm.
1. Baseball—Miscellanea. I. Title.
GV873.B654 2013
796.357—dc23   2012028623

Anchor Trade Paperback ISBN: 978-0-307-95041-3
eBook ISBN: 978-0-385-53613-4

Author photograph © Xanthos / News

www.anchorbooks.com

Printed in the United States of America
10 9 8 7 6 5 4 3 2 1

For Charlotte, LynNell, Larisa, Halley, Sofia, Matilda, and Helen

CONTENTS

WHO'S ON WORST?

INTRODUCTION

THERE ARE A mere 750 active roster spots on the thirty Major League Baseball clubs. There are perhaps a billion people in the United States, Mexico, east Asia, plus Central and South America who would betray best friends and gladly suffer painful, performance-enhancing treatments in order to obtain these lucrative, perk-barreled jobs. If the staggering odds of success were the same in lawyering or sportswriting, most of us now gainfully employed would be unemployed, rejected out of hand as amateurish hacks. So it is a bit unjust, really, to label any Chicago Cub, San Diego Padre, or Kansas City Royal a lousy athlete. These players are the best of the best, or they would quickly be cut adrift. Their hand-eye coordination, their swiftness of foot, and their strength of arm must surely be otherworldly.

And yet, from where we critics sit in the bleachers or in front of our laptops, many of these men are not only mortal; they often appear to be clumsy bunglers. They flub grounders, swing at curveballs in the dirt, get picked off base, drop fly balls, walk batters with the bases loaded, or forget there is only one man out. In a sport that demands smart, spontaneous decision making, these players are at times terrible problem solvers. Baseball is all about failure, we know. Even the greatest of batters bangs out a hit less than 35 percent of the time. Each game is declared finished when players on the losing side produce twenty-seven outs—barring extra innings, in which case they fail even more often. There is no great shame in any of that. But some of these players over the decades have elevated failure, or folly, to fresh, artful levels, which is what this book is all about.

Without these major-league oafs who have made such a hash of the sport, icons such as Willie Mays, Mariano Rivera, and Joe DiMaggio would not glitter quite so brightly. Lesser lights also inspire the rest of us in their own flawed way, make us all dream big-league dreams. If Marv Throneberry, Bob Uecker, Mario Mendoza, and Kei Igawa can achieve professional stature, signing big-league contracts for a season or more, isn't there considerable hope for our children, our grandchildren?

This book examines and ranks these ungainly muses in a number of unique categories. Every major-league ballplayer who ever allowed a passed ball or hurled a double-play relay into the stands becomes a candidate for inclusion. Every coach or owner who blew up a franchise is also eligible. There are some decent players in here, too, if they cheated too often, acted too callously, or merely had the good fortune to be paid way too much for their mediocre services. The better the backstory, the more prominent the entry. Only one caveat: in order to qualify, a fellow needs to have appeared in, or impacted, at least one major-league game during a regular season. No minor-league Michael Jordans allowed.

1 | THE MENDOZA LINE
The Worst Hitters of All Time

HITTING IS A difficult craft, inherently prone to humbling disappointment. But then there are those players who further lower the bar, who aspire desperately to bloop a single every fourth or fifth time at the plate, who ought never have taken bat in hand. Even as baseball evolved from dead-ball to juiced-body eras, some batters always stood out as much worse than those around them. They struggled to cross the Mendoza Line, to remain above that .200 mark and avoid detection.

We don't include pitchers in this category. They are specialists with alibis ready in pocket. All other positions are eligible, however, and most are represented here. Bring us your poor batting averages, your low on-base percentages, your high strikeout-to-walk ratios, your embarrassing WARs (wins above replacement), and your humiliating sabermetrics.

BILL BERGEN AND HIS 0-FOR-45 (46?) SLUMP

Bill Bergen was a catcher for the Brooklyn Superbas in the dead-ball era, when everyone was in a slump of sorts. Still, even by the measure of his day, Bergen set the gold standard for persistent batting ineptitude. While he demonstrated his futility way back in 1909, his achievement lives and breathes today, still fueling controversy as to whether his slump might really have been 0 for 46. Historians have argued among themselves recently whether

one particular handwritten scorecard had him at 0 for 2 in a game or 0 for 3. During an equally impressive slump by Craig Counsell of the Brewers in 2011, *The New York Times* became somewhat obsessed with this statistical debate, running two lengthy stories about Bergen, one a correction of sorts. And when Counsell laced a pinch-hit single at 0 for 45, it meant that the Bergen argument would live another day and remain just as relevant.

Old-timer Bill Bergen was far better behind the plate for Brooklyn than when he was standing next to it, with his lifetime batting average of .170.
Library of Congress

The chief researcher on this subject was Joe Dittmar, vice chairman of the records committee for the Society for American Baseball Research. Dittmar originally determined Bergen's streak was 46, until the Elias Sports Bureau challenged that finding, lowering the number to 45. This meant that another player, Dave Campbell, had tied the mark in 1973 (Campbell managed to bat .000 for the Cardinals that year in twenty-one at-bats, after being traded from the Padres). When Campbell reached 45, nobody even noticed or cared. But in the present-day Stat Age, every hit or miss is quantified, logged, and reexamined. Dittmar went back to check the scorecards again. He discovered one on July 14, 1909, in which the number of Bergen's at-bats was smudged. Upon closer inspection, he believed the number was a 2 and not a 3, lowering Bergen's slump to 0 for 45.

Regardless of the finding, Bergen once made himself a good case for being labeled the very worst hitter in major-league history. He still holds the record for the lowest single-season batting average, .139, for a position player with a qualifying number of at-bats. He also posted the lowest career batting average, .170. He hit a grand total of two home runs in 3,028 career at-bats, with an on-base percentage of only .194 and a slugging percentage—in this case, the stat is a terrible misnomer—of just .201. Though there are no film clips of the fellow, it is safe to say he wasn't the most aggressive batter. Bergen was never struck by a pitch, which would seem to indicate he didn't exactly crowd the plate. A reasonable fan might ask, therefore: How did Bergen manage to draw a paycheck for eleven seasons in the big leagues?

Turns out this is no great mystery. Bergen had a Hall of Fame arm. He was a marvelous defensive catcher, one of the greatest to squat behind the plate. In 941 games, he amassed 1,444 assists, ranking him among the all-time top twenty. He threw out 47.3 percent of runners who tried to steal on his rifle arm. In one truly epic game against the Cards in 1909, Bergen nailed half a dozen base runners.

"He is one of the few backstops who can throw on a line to second while standing flat-footed," wrote a reporter for *The Sporting News* in 1908. "He gets the ball away from him so quickly and with so little apparent exertion that the runner on first, second or third does not dare to take liberties when Billie is on the job."

Bergen also had a terrifying psychological alibi for failing at bat, if he ever wished to employ it. His older brother, Marty, played for the Boston Beaneaters from 1896 to 1899 and was rated a far better player. Then, a year before Bill broke into the league in 1901 with the Cincinnati Reds, Marty Bergen slaughtered his own wife and two children with an ax before committing bloody suicide with a razor blade. Bill was apparently nothing like Marty, who was known to scold teammates while throwing tantrums on and off the field. Marty was considered pathologically paranoid. His brother, Bill, was simply a nice guy with no torque to his swing.

RAY OYLER AND HIS LOYAL FANS

Ray Oyler may well have been the worst hitter in modern baseball, a batter who rarely climbed to that magical .200 mark. He was also living proof, however, that everybody has his time and place. In Oyler's case, that place was Seattle in 1969, when he would become the oddest of cult heroes with the expansion Pilots.

By 1968, in his fourth year with the Tigers as a slick-fielding shortstop, the Detroit fans had grown fed up with Oyler and jeered him from Opening Day. You couldn't really blame them. In his previous three seasons, Oyler batted .186, .171, and .207. He was on his way in 1968 to a batting average of .135, breaking the low-water mark for any player who appeared in a hundred or more games. Oyler's fielding average was fifteen points above the league average for shortstops, but he went literally hitless from July 13 through the end of the season. This was now a terrible hitter in a terrible slump, so the Tigers benched their reliable glove man for the World Series against the Cardinals—replacing him with Mickey Stanley, an outfielder. Oyler entered four World Series games as a late defensive replacement and was permitted to come to the plate only once, to lay down a sacrifice bunt. The Tigers won the championship and then left Oyler unprotected in the expansion draft. The Pilots selected him in the fifth round.

It was here, in Seattle, that Oyler became an instant hero, thanks in good part to the radio personality Robert E. Lee Hardwick, whose ramblings were aired on the Pilots' station, KVI.

Hardwick recognized the irony in starting a fan club for this particularly bat-challenged player. The comedy show *Laugh-In* was a big hit at the time on NBC, heavily dosed with the signature catchphrase "Sock it to me." Hardwick called his new fan club by the acronym "SOC IT TO ME .300." Those letters stood for "Slugger Oyler Can, In Time, Top Our Manager's Estimate" and hit .300. The city of Seattle was simply thrilled to get a major-league team, and Oyler became something of a cherished mascot. "He started it just to drum up a little interest in the Seattle club," Oyler said of Hardwick. "So I figured, what the heck, 150 or 200 members would be a nice thing. But now it's up to 10,000 and they say it's still climbing." Eventually, about 15,000 fans joined the club. Oyler, who was earning $18,800 that season, was given a free apartment and a car. Then, on Opening Day at Sicks Stadium, before Oyler had ever swung and missed at a fastball, the fan club gave him a wild welcome. "He got cheers, horns blew, confetti filled the air in his first time at bat," wrote the author Fred Cavinder.

Oyler responded to this hysteria with a hit, then won the next game with a homer as his average spiked at .364. "It's a great feeling," Oyler said. "Even when you make an out, they start cheering you." Unfortunately, his average was down to .220 by May, to .190 by June, to .176 by July, to .163 by August, and to .161 by September. Still, Oyler was cheered, and he insisted, "I'm hitting the ball good at home. I've got four home runs there." A single against Oakland on the last day of the season lifted his average to .165, as the Pilots finished 64-98, dead last and thirty-three games behind the Twins in the newly formed American League West. Even Oyler's fielding average that season of .965 was below par, by his high standards.

Unfortunately for Oyler, the Pilots were in worse shape than his batting average. They were acquired in bankruptcy by Bud Selig, who moved them to Milwaukee for the 1970 season, where they became the Brewers. The people of Milwaukee did not have an emotional investment in Oyler's career, so he was traded before the season to Oakland, then signed by California for a twenty-four-game stint in 1970 in which he batted .083 with a perfect fielding percentage. After he retired, Oyler opened a bowling alley in the Seattle area, where he was still beloved and where three strikes in a row were considered a good thing.

BOB UECKER, BALLPARK COMIC

Many players before and after Bob Uecker have been equally disparaged, but none has embraced the tag of incompetence with such inspiration or mercenary zeal. Uecker somehow managed to forge an entire self-deprecating career from six seasons as a utility catcher with four teams from 1962 to 1967. When the infield dust settled, he finished with 167 strikeouts in 731 at-bats and a batting average of precisely .200. This serendipitous statistic is one that Uecker was able to exploit brilliantly in his role as Brewers announcer, film actor, wrestling emcee, and stand-up comedian. As Uecker put it, "I had slumps that lasted into winter." By his own account, Uecker's greatest achievement was receiving an intentional walk from Sandy Koufax, with first base open and the pitcher on deck. When he was traded to St. Louis from his hometown Milwaukee Braves at the start of the 1964 season, the deal was for a utility catcher, Gary Kolb, who finished with a career .209 batting average—which meant that still, somehow, it had been a good trade for the Braves.

It is impossible to poke fun at Uecker's career with less mercy or greater wit than the man did himself. Over time, his career in retrospect became one long nightclub skit. Speaking about a $3,000 signing bonus with the Braves, Uecker almost didn't accept the proposal, because, he said, "My old man didn't have that kind of money to put out." His managers supposedly told him, "Grab a bat and stop this rally." When he took his kids to

Bob Uecker, baseball's clown prince, was always
out of tune in the batter's box. *AP Photo*

a game, he said, "They'd want to come home with a different
player."

Uecker was ironically dubbed Mr. Baseball by Johnny Carson,
one of the first television talk show hosts to appreciate his tale-
telling talents and sense of comic timing. The Milwaukee-born-
and-based player morphed into a well-known self-satirist with
the help of Miller Lite commercials. In one of those ads, Uecker
is ushered to a ballpark seat far, far away from the front row,
where he smugly expected to land. To this day, the obstructed
top-level seats at Miller Park in Milwaukee are known as Uecker
seats.

Uecker, by the way, wasn't quite as terrible defensively, which he never wanted you to know. He committed few errors while throwing out one-third of base stealers, a respectable stat. He did allow forty-seven passed balls in 271 games, including a league-leading twenty-seven passed balls in 1967 when he was forced to catch the knuckleballer Phil Niekro. Uecker's oft-cited quip on the best way to catch the knuckler: "Wait'll it stops rolling, then go pick it up."

MARIO MENDOZA, THE MAN AND THE LINE

Long before the Internet made even the most obscure baseball statistics available to Bill James freaks at the flick of an index finger, fans relied on the Sunday sports section to provide them with their numerical fix. Most dailies would list in agate type the batting averages of every player in the majors who had amassed enough plate appearances to qualify for consideration. Most often, these averages were listed from best to worst. It was because of this feature—and the playful minds belonging to the Hall of Famer George Brett and the ESPN broadcaster Chris Berman—that Mario Mendoza became much more than just another forgettable, retired journeyman with a lilting name. Brett was in the news regularly, flirting with the .400 mark in 1980, when he said in an interview, "The first thing I look for in the Sunday papers is who is below the Mendoza Line." According to a *Sports Illustrated* piece on the subject, it was actually a pair of Mendoza's teammates on Seattle, Tom Paciorek and Bruce Bochte, who first joked about that imaginary line in an interview before Brett picked up on it. Mendoza, a Mariners shortstop at the time, had laid down the baseline for terrible hitting with his .200-ish average nearly every season. Berman heard Brett's quote and ran with it. Soon every player off to a slow start or suffering through a lengthy slump was being judged in comparison to this Mendoza Line. "That is all people remember me for," Mendoza lamented years later.

To be fair, Mendoza did not finish his career at the Mendoza Line. He had a .215 career batting average after hitting .245—with two homers!—in 1980, the season when Brett and Berman made him famous. The player always felt he might have fared better if he hadn't been lifted so often for pinch hitters. "It made it hard," Mendoza told BaseballNation.net. "If I could have gotten to the plate three or four times a game, I could have made better adjustments." Mendoza landed under the Mendoza Line in five of his nine seasons and finished at .118 during his farewell year, 1982, in Texas. The 1979 season was probably his signature year, and the one that stuck in Brett's mind. Mendoza hit .198 with one homer in 373 at-bats that season, striking out sixty-two times.

For those who cared to dig a bit deeper, Mario Mendoza Aizpuru was more than just a pundit's concoction. His baseball career was long and eventful. Born in Chihuahua, he was one of the first Mexican players in the majors and was later elected to the Mexican Hall of Fame. Mendoza recalled how one African-American teammate once told him, "You're not black, you're not white, you're orange." He was playing for the Mexico City Red Devils of the Mexican League in 1970 when a Pirate scout spotted his fielding exploits, ignored the batting flaws, and signed Mendoza to a contract. His nickname in Mexico had nothing to do with any imaginary line. He was called Manos de Seda, or "Silk Hands," for his uncanny ability to pluck low, hard grounders off the infield dirt.

After four seasons in the minors, Mendoza made his debut in 1974 as a ninth-inning pinch runner for the lumbering Willie Stargell. He scored, too. Mendoza could run and he could throw. On June 28, 1977, his arm was put to the ultimate test. The Pirates' manager, Chuck Tanner, was badly strapped for pitchers in the second game of the team's second doubleheader in three days. Down 10–3 in the nightcap, Mendoza was brought in to pitch a couple of innings. Unfortunately, he wasn't pitching against himself. He fared fine for a while, getting Keith Hernandez to line into a double play. His second inning did not go as well. Ken Reitz laced a three-run homer, leaving Mendoza with a 13.50 career earned run average.

Mendoza's lack of hitting prowess did not prevent him from becoming a coach with the Hawaii Islanders and then player-manager of the Monclova Acereros in Mexico. He batted .291 in the Mexican League, where he was immensely popular and became known by a different nickname, Elegante. When he was done with that, Mendoza was hired to manage the Angels' Single-A farm club, the Lake Elsinore Storm, where he coached his son, Mario junior. The son, after watching his dad's exploits at the plate, had decided to become a pitcher.

JOHN GOCHNAUR, NO-HIT, NO-FIELD

Any statistical argument about the worst player in the history of baseball inevitably leads at some point to John Gochnaur, a pioneer in the sport whose bat and glove together marked him, at the very least, as the worst of the early-timers. If not for the brevity of service, his credentials for that dishonor would be impeccable. In 264 games and three seasons from 1901 to 1903 with the Brooklyn Superbas and the Cleveland Broncos and Naps, Gochnaur batted .187 with no homers and with 146 errors at shortstop. In his final, signature year, Gochnaur hit .185 with an astounding 98 errors in 134 games. Admittedly, the league fielding percentage in this 1903 season was only .913, but even by those standards Gochnaur's .869 stood out in the wrong way. As for his batting average, the typical player of his time was hitting .270, leaving Gochnaur .085 short.

Gochnaur was born and raised in Altoona, Pennsylvania, then followed his dream at the age of twenty, traveling around the country playing minor-league ball in Virginia, Maryland, Massachusetts, New Jersey, and Ohio. After a couple of decent seasons as a second baseman for the Dayton Old Soldiers of the Western Association, Gochnaur was hired by the Brooklyn Superbas in 1901 as a shortstop. From there, it was all downhill, in a hurry. Undeterred by his failures in Brooklyn and Cleveland, Gochnaur continued his career in the minors for five more years. Against Class A pitching, he would bat .161, .156, .199, and .199. In 1907, his last season in Des Moines of the Western League, Gochnaur somehow went out in a relative blaze of glory, batting a hefty .260 with 109 hits in 420 at-bats.

The baseball author and historian Mike Attiyeh rightfully gets credit for unearthing and researching Gochnaur's otherwise anonymous career. Attiyeh found Gochnaur to be "a popular man and a friend to many ballplayers." A lifelong bachelor called simply Goch by friends, Gochnaur was a local institution in Altoona and helped hundreds of area players secure contracts with minor-league teams. An *Altoona Mirror* article reported that he worked at different times as a city police officer, a Penn railroad policeman, and a bartender. As for Gochnaur's baseball career, Attiyeh came to this conclusion: "Few have been worse than Gochnaur with the bat and fewer still might have been worse than Gochnaur in the field, but none combined the two-way futility quite the way Gochnaur did."

Gochnaur's legend lives on in popular culture. A Utah congressman, Rob Bishop, gave a speech to the House of Representatives in which he attacked the Endangered Species Act in 2005 by comparing its efficacy to that of Gochnaur's playing career. Five years later, in a television episode of *Bones,* the character Arastoo Vaziri, a lab assistant, referred to Gochnaur as the "worst baseball player ever." If only he'd put in a few more bad seasons in the major leagues, that distinction would be undisputed.

BOTTOM TEN

1   **BILL BERGEN**   Sure, they can tie his hitless streak, but can anyone break it?

2   **RAY OYLER**   Gets major credit for that .135 Season.

3   **BOB UECKER**   He'd like to be No. 1.

4   **J. R. PHILLIPS**   Career batting average of .188 with four teams, striking out 180 times in 501 at-bats.

5   **MARIO MENDOZA**   Lilting name, ugly swing.

6   **JOHN GOCHNAUR**   Just terrible, all around.

7   **RAFAEL BELLIARD**   In seventeen seasons, he smacked two homers and seventy-one extra base hits.

8   **JOHNNIE LEMASTER**   A .222 career hitter who was jeered so much he wore a jersey with "BOO" on the back.

9   **DAVE WAYNE ROBERTS**   Hit .167 in 1974 with the Padres.

10   **JIM "GRASSHOPPER" LILLIE**   Batted .175 with zero homers and a slugging percentage of .197 in 1886 for the Kansas City Cowboys.

2 | HOBSON'S DISEASE
The Worst Fielders of All Time

THE INVENTION OF the designated hitter was a gift from the baseball gods to all American League klutzes, who suddenly were not required to stumble out of the dugout and pretend to man any position. Unfortunately, this merciful exemption was not in effect until 1973 and still has not been extended to National Leaguers. Therefore, baseball is littered through the ages with tales and videotapes of unrequited glove, of outrageous catching and throwing errors by players who were all bat, no mitt. Some of those errors came at particularly inopportune moments, rendering them even more infamous. The very worst fielders, though, were consistently awful, botching grounders on large and small occasions.

DICK STUART AND HIS STRANGE GLOVE

Dick Stuart was a god-awful fielder and never bothered denying it. He enjoyed his nickname, Dr. Strangeglove, and even sported a custom license plate for his car that bragged, "E-3." Despite and because of his shortcomings, Stuart played for six different teams over ten seasons and eleven years, from 1958 to 1969. If the designated hitter spot had existed then, Stuart's career might have endured longer and his offensive stats grown even more impressive. But there was nowhere to hide, and Stuart somehow managed to commit twenty-nine errors at first base in 1963, still a major-league record for that position.

Stuart was a prodigious hitter from the start, knocking sixty-six homers in 1956 for the Lincoln Chiefs, a Class A minor-league club. But even as he was busy signing autographs with "Dick Stuart 66," his reputation as an impossibly lousy fielder postponed his promotion to the Pirates. "Dick Stuart is the worst outfielder I ever saw in my life," Pittsburgh's manager, Bobby Bragan, declared, explaining his reluctance to give the kid a chance.

Bragan wasn't around when Stuart finally got his shot with the Pirates as a mid-season call-up in 1958. The new manager, Danny Murtaugh, moved him to first base, the position Stuart would butcher for the remainder of his career with the Pirates, Red Sox, Phillies, Mets, Dodgers, and Angels. In his first game, played at Wrigley Field, Stuart homered. In his second game there, he ripped a grand slam. But while Stuart totaled sixteen homers in just sixty-seven games that first season, he also committed sixteen errors. There was never anything subtle about Stuart's skills. He was a big guy, six feet two inches and 212 pounds, with a big swing. He amassed 228 homers with 743 RBIs and a .489 slugging average, while striking out 957 times in 3,997 at-bats. In the field, he quickly became a running joke. He was once given a standing ovation when he scooped up a loose hot dog wrapper blowing around first base. After a crowd at spring training was warned not to interfere with the ball in play, Murtaugh quipped, "I hope Stuart doesn't think that means him."

Before Stuart hung up his rebellious mitt, he experienced several notable adventures. He was on deck waiting to pinch-hit when Bill Mazeroski won Game 7 of the 1960 World Series with a ninth-inning homer off Ralph Terry of the Yankees. "I was kneeling in the on-deck circle, thinking I was going to be the hero," Stuart said. "And all of a sudden, I was out on the field jumping around." After his power numbers and batting average slipped in 1966, Stuart was released by the Dodgers at age thirty-three. Instead of retiring, he took his big bat to the Taiyo Whales in Japan for two seasons. There, he enjoyed only mixed success and was actually benched at times by yet another manager who couldn't stomach his defensive shortcomings. Stuart, however, insisted the benching had nothing to do with that. "The manager was in the Japanese air force in World War II and didn't like Americans," Stuart told the Philadelphia *Bulletin*. More likely, it was the glove. "Everybody liked Dick," said Dick Schofield, a former Pirates teammate. "But he did have trouble with that leather thing."

SMEAD JOLLEY AND THE HOLE IN HIS MITT

Smead Jolley was such a bad fielder that a .305 career batting average and a .475 slugging percentage couldn't keep him in the major leagues for more than four seasons. Every scout knew about Jolley's shortcomings from the start, but after he posted full seasons in the minors batting .404 and .387, he was given a chance. From 1930 to 1933, the White Sox and the Red Sox tried to hide "Smudge" in left or right field—never in center—to no avail. He might have thrived in an era of the designated hitter, but alas there was no such shelter. Jolley committed forty-four errors in just 811 chances, and it got so bad that Chicago gave up on him, dealing him to Boston during a 1932 season when he would hit .312 with eighteen homers and 106 RBIs.

Jolley was still only thirty-one years old when the Red Sox traded him to the St. Louis Browns, who turned around immediately and traded him to a minor-league club, the Hollywood Stars of the Pacific Coast League. This might have discouraged most men, but Jolley knew he could still hit and kept at it for eight more seasons in the minors. His batting averages at these Class AA, A, and B stops were extremely gaudy. He hit .360, .372, and .373 from 1934 to 1936 in Hollywood and Albany, yet still no major-league club would have a part of him because of his mitt.

Jolley's most astounding exploit, however, was yet to come. In 1937, he played for the Nashville Volunteers of the Southern Association in a quirky stadium called Sulphur Dell. Here, right field was built on a hill with a slope that started behind first base and climbed about twenty-five feet high to the base of the shallow fence. Right fielders there were called mountain goats and generally played their position near the wall so they could run down the hill to catch fly balls, rather than up. Placing a horrid fielder like Jolley in such a position was asking for trouble, and then one day he botched a play in a historic manner. Jolley supposedly ran down the right field hill to cut off a simple ground-ball single. The baseball skipped between his legs and bounced up the hill to the wall, allowing the runner to reach second base. Jolley ran back to retrieve the ball, but it bounced off the fence and whizzed past him a second time, back down the hill, allowing the runner to claim third. Jolley then chugged down the hill, picked up the ball, missed the cutoff man, and overthrew the catcher. The batter scored, and Jolley was reportedly charged with two fielding errors, plus one throwing error on a single play. The only other three-error play cited in professional baseball history arrived many years later, in 1988, when the pitcher Tommy John bungled a grounder, threw away the ball, then bobbled the relay throw from right field and threw wildly to home plate. The scoring on Jolley's play may be apocryphal, because official records show he committed only three errors total that year in Nashville, and it is unlikely he made no others.

Give Jolley some credit, though. He never stopped hitting. During those minor-league years, even at age thirty-nine in 1941, playing for the Spokane Indians and the Vancouver Capilanos of the Western International League, Jolley batted .345 in a full, 133-game season. He also made only seven errors in 185 chances, which was pretty good by his standards.

BUTCH HOBSON AND HIS BAD AIM

Hard to believe, but Clell Lavern "Butch" Hobson's wayward arm—the one that whipped throws from third base into the Fenway stands and bopped spectators behind first with alarming regularity—once hurled passes for Bear Bryant at Alabama. Hobson, Tuscaloosa-born, quarterbacked the Crimson Tide before he was drafted by the Red Sox, an indication of just how accurately that arm once performed. It might also be a reason the limb deteriorated from overuse and contributed to forty-three errors in 1978.

Hobson was still faring fine in 1977, a sheer hustler with a powerful swing, until his right elbow began misbehaving toward the close of that thirty-homer, 112-RBI season. Hobson foolishly did nothing about the bone chips over the winter, and then in 1978 the arm fell off its hinges. "That was stupidity, not having [surgery] done when I should have had it done," Hobson later told *The Boston Globe*. His self-prescribed treatment was, "Let's take some pain killers and go home and drink more beer. And get up the next day and do whatever we got to do."

The result of such negligence was an ugly series of errors and clumsy attempts to compensate for them. Hobson would field a grounder neatly enough, then stagger through one or two false starts toward first before finally talking himself into releasing the baseball, which rarely heeded its launch instructions. As his teammate the pitcher Bill Lee said, "His arm was a dogleg right."

His syndrome, dubbed Hobson's Disease by the unsympathetic masses, became as much a mental block as it was a physical disability. To complicate matters, this was no ordinary season he'd picked for the meltdown. The Red Sox were in the midst of a nosedive and an ill-fated scramble with the Yankees. Both teams would finish at 99-63, setting up the playoff game decided by Bucky Dent's homer. Any one of Hobson's errors could be blamed for blowing the big August lead and for his team's eventual demise. Hobson had already collected his forty-three errors—about twenty-nine of them throwing errors—with three weeks left in the season, when he finally informed Don Zimmer, the manager, he could no longer handle third base duties. Zimmer, enamored of Hobson's gung-ho, go-for-broke attitude, otherwise had no intention of benching him. There had been too many good times, like when Hobson ran right through the catcher Rick Dempsey for an inside-the-park homer in June 1976, during his second game ever at Fenway Park. Zimmer and all of Boston had fallen immediately in love with the guy. But this was no longer that Hobson. When he completed his 1978 season with an .899 fielding percentage, it was the first time in sixty years that a regular position player finished under .900.

After aborted stints with the Angels and the Yankees, Hobson finished in the majors with 138 errors in 651 games, or one in every 4.72 games. By comparison, Brooks Robinson committed 264 errors in 2,900 games, or one in every 10.98 games. Hobson never gave up hope of recovering his compass. When the Yanks assigned his woeful arm to the minors in Columbus, he warmed up pitchers and did whatever he could to stay near the game. He was eventually named the Red Sox manager for an unsuccessful three-year stint. He had some trouble with drugs, which he partly blamed on the painkillers. Years later, Hobson still couldn't fully extend his arm, which ached nearly as much as it did to view the clips.

MARVELOUS MARV THRONEBERRY

There is no more lilting, poetic appellation for systemic baseball failure than Marvelous Marv. It is even difficult to assign
Throneberry a category in this book, because he was one of the
great twin threats of all time. He was both a terrible base runner and a horrific first baseman. He managed to butcher these
two crafts with such artful imagination that he quickly became
a cult figure in New York, inspiring a large fan club of his own,
the VRAM—Marv spelled backward. This was back with the
original Mets of 1962, arguably the worst baseball team in the
modern era, with a record of 40-120. Consider that the infield of
Throneberry, Hot Rod Kanehl, Félix Mantilla, and Charlie Neal
combined for ninety-six errors in that single season, a feat that
still appears on paper nearly impossible. And when Throneberry sat, ancient Gil Hodges, thirty-eight years old at the time,
added five errors in reserve. So this was, indeed, a special group,
destined to make bad history. Yet Throneberry somehow managed to stand out as especially awful, even among these peers.
He was the crown jewel in the tiara of ineptitude. In his classic book on that Mets team, *Can't Anybody Here Play This Game?*,
Jimmy Breslin wrote, "Marvelous Marv was holding down first
base. This is like saying Willie Sutton works at your bank."

Throneberry came to the Mets by way of the Orioles early in
the 1962 season and still found the time to commit seventeen
errors at first base in just 97 games. For the purpose of comparison, Mark Teixeira made four errors in 147 games during 2011 at
the same position for the Yankees.

It wasn't just the official errors, the dropped balls, or the wild
throws that rendered Throneberry so endearing. Of particular
amusement were his rundown misplays, when a Mets pitcher
had picked off one of the many runners to reach base against

If Marvelous Marv Throneberry caught a ball at first
base, it was usually by accident. *AP Photo*

this team. As Breslin put it, in understated fashion, "Rundowns
are not Throneberry's strong suit." In one incident, Throneberry
was paralyzed by confusion while standing in the base path and
without the ball. He thus allowed Don Landrum of the Cubs to
virtually leap into his arms for an interference call. In another
episode, recounted by Breslin, Throneberry earnestly attempted
to run down Ken Boyer of the Cards from first to second base,
ignoring the bigger picture, permitting Stan Musial to score the
winning run from third.

If Throneberry was a disaster in the field, he was an equally
creative saboteur as a runner. In a June game against the Chicago
Cubs, he briefly became a hero after hitting a game-winning triple with two outs and the bases loaded. Unfortunately, he quite

obviously missed touching first base. It wasn't even close. The Cubs appealed, the umpire called out Throneberry, and the runs were voided. Casey Stengel stormed out of the dugout to argue the call but was told by the ump, "Casey, I hate to tell you this, but he also missed second."

Stengel once said, "When you're losing, you commence to play stupid." The manager should probably have known better than to have included this likable klutz on his roster. Throneberry had already played briefly for Stengel under very different circumstances with the 1958 Yankees, after signing out of South Side High in Memphis, Tennessee. He even got one World Series at-bat. But he didn't play much with the Yanks or the Orioles, and the Mets' GM, George Weiss, thought Throneberry still had considerable upside. Unfortunately, this opportunity for Throneberry to play regularly, the baseball reporter Leonard Shecter wrote, "revealed him."

"Throneberry, 29 at the time, looked much older," Shecter wrote. "He was thickly built and his bald head was covered with freckles. He was from a small town in Tennessee, chewed tobacco and had a country accent." Throneberry didn't fit in, and he was booed at first for his misplays. Slowly, surely, with the help of Richie Ashburn in the neighboring locker, Throneberry learned to revel in his own misdeeds. By the time he was traded the next season to make room for Ed Kranepool, he had become a lovable institution. Before he died in 1994 at age sixty of cancer, Throneberry was asked to join the likes of Bob Uecker in self-deprecating Miller Lite commercials. His recurring line, "I still don't know why they asked me to do this commercial," became something of a comedic catchphrase. Throneberry looked utterly and naturally out of place, just as he had around the infield. And once again, it worked for him.

CHUCK KNOBLAUCH AND THE YIPS

Chuck Knoblauch wasn't always a car wreck at second base. He enjoyed a relatively seamless early career, drafted out of Texas A&M to become American League Rookie of the Year in 1991. He was a postseason standout that October, helping the Twins capture the World Series and making one particularly heads-up defensive play in Game 7. Knoblauch feigned a double-play relay at second on a clean double by Terry Pendleton of the Braves. Lonnie Smith, advancing on a hit-and-run from first base, slowed down and did not score on the play, a critical moment in the 1–0, ten-inning victory for Minnesota. During 1997, Knoblauch's final season with the Minnesota Twins, he was awarded the Gold Glove to go with his All-Star selection.

Despite his popularity in Minneapolis and a five-year, $30 million contract extension, Knoblauch became demoralized by the Twins' failings in the standings and demanded a trade. "The losing got to me," he said. He was traded in 1998 for $3 million and four players to the Bronx, where Knoblauch was set to become the long-term, clockwork infield partner of Derek Jeter. What happened next was very difficult to watch. Knoblauch's muscle memory failed him terribly, as did his baseball wits. The same player who was making such smart decisions in Minnesota showed signs of fraying. In a 1998 American League Championship Series game, Knoblauch argued an umpire's decision without first calling time-out, allowing a runner, Enrique Wilson, to score all the way from first base for the go-ahead run. The New York *Daily News* immediately labeled him "BLAUCH-HEAD" on it's back page. Worse, Knoblauch persistently made wild throws to first base from the fifteen or twenty yards that separate a second baseman from the bag. In 1998, he committed thirteen errors in 149 games. In 1999, those misplays increased to twenty-six while his fielding percentage plummeted to .963.

His total fielding runs above average, according to Baseball Projection.com, went from 17 in 1997 to –15 just two years later.

"Something obviously went wrong, but I have no idea what it was," Knoblauch would tell the Minneapolis *Star Tribune* years later. "I got to thinking too much and I couldn't shut it off. It was bright lights, big city and I was having this serious issue

in front of millions of people and I had to wake up every day and face it. And I faced it. If you care so much about something, it's hard not to make it a life and death thing. I feel like I went to New York as a boy and I left it a man. Because I went through the wringer."

By 2000, Knoblauch's fielding percentage had dipped to an embarrassing .958, and he was being employed more often as a designated hitter. All the drills and advice did not help. His low point arrived in June of that season. Despite a pep talk from his mom and sympathetic ovations from fans, Knoblauch whipped a fourth errant toss

Duck and cover! Chuck Knoblauch is throwing toward first base, and likely beyond. *AP Photo/Eric Draper*

in three games, striking the mother of the broadcast celebrity Keith Olbermann in the face with the ball, making unnecessarily large headlines. Olbermann's mother had been sitting seven rows behind first base. The second baseman did not even attempt a double-play relay later in the same game, wisely holding on to the ball.

Knoblauch's case closely resembled that of Steve Sax, a solid second baseman for the Dodgers in the 1980s who suddenly found it nearly impossible to throw the ball accurately to first. Eventually, in 2001, Knoblauch was shifted by Joe Torre to left field in the final year of his contract with the Yanks. Although he was no disaster at the plate, and was part of three championship teams, Knoblauch never approached the kind of offensive production he had enjoyed with the Twins.

Knoblauch retired after one last major-league season in 2002 with Kansas City, though there were more problems to come. *The Mitchell Report*, released in 2007, conveyed that Knoblauch had obtained human growth hormones in 2001 from the assistant strength coach Kirk Radomski while with the Yankees. Although Knoblauch refused to meet with investigators, he later admitted, unapologetically, to using the performance-enhancing drug. "I did HGH," Knoblauch said. "It didn't help me out. It didn't make me any better. I had the worst years of my career from a batting average standpoint. And I got hurt. So there was no good that came out of it for me—it was not performance-enhancing for me."

BOTTOM TEN

1   **DICK STUART**   Twenty-nine errors at first base in a single season.

2   **SMEAD JOLLEY**   Did he really commit three errors on one play?

3   **BUTCH HOBSON**   Arm like a sprinkler system.

4   **MARV THRONEBERRY**   The most Amazin' Met.

5   **CURT BLEFARY**   Outfielder nicknamed Clank by his teammate Frank Robinson.

6   **CHUCK KNOBLAUCH**   Watch out, Mrs. Olbermann.

7   **JOSÉ CANSECO**   He used his head as a trampoline, and the baseball jumped for a homer.

8   **GREG LUZINSKI**   In sabermetrics terms, he cost the Phils and the Chisox ninety-three total runs (Rtot) on defense over his career.

9   **STEVE SAX**   Went from Rookie of the Year in 1982 to thirty errors in 1983.

10   **FRANK HOWARD**   His last season was first year of DH; could have used many more.

3 | LIMA TIME!
The Worst Pitchers of All Time

A **PITCHER CAN BOMB** in any number of fashions. He can be wild. He can lose his fastball. His sinker can stop sinking. He can choke under pressure. He can give in to the batter on a 2-2 count. No matter what the path, failure on the mound is arguably the most ego-crushing experience in baseball. A pitcher stands alone out there, armed only with his stuff and a signal from the catcher. When his pitches sail off target, when the bullpen is alerted to start stretching exercises, there is no escape from the eyes of impatient thousands.

A batter is expected to fail most of the time. Those same percentages shift the burden of probable success onto the pitcher. Yet whenever he and his peers succeed too often, the geometry of the game is adjusted accordingly. The mound is lowered. The baseball itself mysteriously grows livelier. Or more nefariously, batters ingest illegal elixirs that tilt the balance. Historically, conditions are stacked against even the best arms in the major leagues. Pity the worst ones, who are overmatched from the start.

HERM WEHMEIER, WILD THING

Nobody should throw wild pitches too close to home. Herm Wehmeier's experience in Cincinnati became a cautionary tale about a local hero who might have fared far better plying his erratic talents far away from his hometown, or perhaps tried a different vocation. "Big Herm" was a three-sport superstar at Western Hills High School but turned down several football scholarship offers to sign with the Reds in 1945. He had amassed a 45-2 record in high school in American Legion games. When the Reds promoted him from the minors that September at age eighteen, Wehmeier gave them a taste of what was to come: in two games, over just five innings, he gave up ten hits, four walks, and seven runs. It was the very first outing, Wehmeier said, that broke his heart.

"Bill McKechnie was our manager but he had been called home. Jimmy Wilson ran the ball club and started me against the Giants," Wehmeier would tell Arthur Daley of *The New York Times* years later. "I had them beaten, 5–2, through the fifth. Then Jimmy yanked me for a pinch hitter. Why? I dunno. He never said and I never asked him. So I sat on the bench while the Giants rallied to beat us, 8–5. Nothing ever has come easy for me in this business."

Undeterred, the Reds made him part of their starting rotation in 1948 and stuck with him for most of the next five seasons. The trouble wasn't Wehmeier's stuff or his talent. "Wehmeier was one of the finest natural athletes we ever had in Cincinnati," said Gabe Paul, the former Reds' general manager. The problem, at least during the first half of his career, was control. Wehmeier led the majors in walks during three seasons, in wild pitches twice, and in hit batsmen once. In 1950, he gave up a whopping 135 walks in 230 innings while allowing a league-high 145 earned runs and finishing with a 5.67 ERA. On May 21, 1950, Wehmeier walked nine Brooklyn Dodgers, gave up nine earned runs, and still somehow was allowed to throw a complete game while getting credited with the 10–9 victory. Clearly, times have changed.

Herm Wehmeier, wild on the mound, was domesticated around his wife, Sue. *AP Photo/Preston Stroup*

Still, one thing was the same in 1950 as it is today: wild pitchers drove spectators crazy. As he unraveled on the mound, Wehmeier was mercilessly jeered by the same hometown fans who had seen him evolve from high school hero into major leaguer. Dick Drott, another Cincinnati kid who would go on to pitch for the Cubs and the Astros, grew up watching this ordeal in Crosley Field and was horrified. "I never wanted to pitch for the hometown team after seeing what happened to Wehmeier," Drott said. "The Cincinnati fans would stand and boo him for hours. That was low. I know. I was there, and I didn't want the same thing to happen to me."

Wehmeier pitched a total of nine seasons and more than a thousand innings in Cincinnati, despite an ERA of 5.25. He was purchased by Philadelphia midway through the 1954 season, traded to St. Louis in 1956, and sold to Detroit in 1958. He lasted thirteen years in the majors. To be fair, Wehmeier had a couple of decent seasons with the Cardinals as his wildness diminished. In 1956, spared the oversight of his hometown, he won twelve games and threw only two wild pitches in 190⅔ innings. "You've gotta learn to pitch," the St. Louis pitching coach Bill Posedel had scolded him. Part of Wehmeier's success that season was a new high-kick delivery that masked his pitches. Chastened and wiser, he would later become a scout for the Reds in search of prospects with a semblance of control.

TODD VAN POPPEL AND THE FASTBALL THAT DIDN'T MOVE

Todd Van Poppel was once a hot rookie pitching prospect who in the end labored with six teams from 1991 to 2004. But he was much more than that. Van Poppel came to represent everything that was wrong with hotshot kids and with scouting systems that live and die by the radar gun.

Van Poppel was a stud at Martin High School in Arlington, Texas. As a senior, he went 11-3 with a 0.97 ERA and 170 strikeouts. The Atlanta Braves were hugely impressed by his fastball and were seriously considering him as the No. 1 draft pick overall in 1990. But Van Poppel had the audacity to tell the Braves not to draft him, threatening to hold out if they did. Atlanta instead settled for a consolation prize named Chipper Jones. Meanwhile, Van Poppel dropped to the No. 14 pick, where the Oakland A's had promised to sign him immediately to a major-league contract, making him instantly wealthy with a $600,000 bonus.

There were great hopes for Van Poppel when he took the mound in July 1990 at Medford, Oregon, for the Class A Southern Oregon A's. The weather was blazing, a hundred degrees, and it seemed Van Poppel's fastball was nearly as hot. His pitches were clocked at ninety-four miles per hour, and Wes Stock, the A's minor-league pitching instructor, told reporters of the eighteen-year-old prospect, "He's got a nice, loose arm when he's out in front of the count." He struck out five and gave up just one infield hit over three and two-thirds innings against the Bend Bucks.

Soon, however, it became clear that Van Poppel's premature major-league contract was not helping his career. The A's had only limited minor-league options on Van Poppel. They couldn't keep him down on the farm, where he belonged. He started only thirty-two minor-league games over four seasons and was hurt for much of 1992. Van Poppel's flat fastball, devoid of late movement, didn't fool batters for long.

In his lucrative eleven-season career span in the majors, Van Poppel was 40-52, never won more than seven games in a year, and lost several years due to injury. His performance ranged from horrendous (a 9.06 ERA in 1996) to merely bad (an ERA of 5.45 or higher from 2002 to 2004). Yet somehow Van Poppel, with his 40-52 record and his 5.58 career ERA, earned more than $8 million, a considerable sum for that—or any other—era.

It didn't help the A's image at the time that Van Poppel was one of four starting pitchers turned flameouts chosen by the team among the first thirty-six picks of that 1990 draft. The media had dubbed this quartet the Four Aces—they were Van Poppel, Don Peters, Kirk Dressendorfer, and Dave Zancanaro— yet only Van Poppel and Dressendorfer ever reached the majors. Dressendorfer managed a grand total of only three victories. Their failures led, indirectly at least, to the later reign of Billy Beane and Moneyball.

Eventually, Van Poppel found his aim, of sorts. In retirement, he hunted on his nine-hundred-acre ranch in Meridian, Texas, and told *The Dallas Morning News* in 2011, "I'm three-for-three on turkeys with my muzzle-loading shotgun." He didn't require much movement on those shots.

CRAZY SCHMIT AND THE NOTEPAD

These days, bookish pitchers study video clips of opposing batters on laptops and iPads before games, searching for wheelhouses to avoid and weaknesses to exploit. But back in 1890, when Frederick "Crazy" Schmit was pitching, there were no such electronic options. So Schmit took it upon himself to compile his own list in a notebook. This in itself might be considered praiseworthy, except for a couple of problems: not blessed with a good memory, the lefty starter quite often pulled out his notebook on the mound and began reading out there, delaying games. By some accounts, he would carefully turn to a page, discover that Honus Wagner or Cap Anson was a very good hitter with few weaknesses, and then decide to walk him intentionally. Schmit also wasn't very good at heeding his own instructions, judging by sheer performance. In five seasons with four teams, he compiled a 5.45 ERA, walking 185 batters while striking out only ninety-three in 361⅓ innings.

Schmit was called Crazy by virtually everyone, an indication of his reputation at the time. He was a big, muscular man. When he got mad, he would often cross his own catcher, throwing his fastest stuff at the plate despite a call for a changeup. Schmit had another nickname less often used, "Germany," referring to his family background. He reportedly spoke with an accent, though it is unclear whether it was natural or affected.

In his travels, Schmit had the distinction of pitching for arguably the worst team in the history of professional baseball, the 1899 Cleveland Spiders of the National League, who posted a 20-134 mark. Their team batting average, .253, was nineteen points lower than that of the second-worst team at the time. But it was their pitching that truly distinguished them as awful. Their ace at the time, Coldwater Hughey, was 4-30 with a 5.41 ERA.

The club's ERA was 6.37. The league average was 3.85. Whenever a Spider showed any promise at all, he was shipped to the
St. Louis Perfectos, a better club owned by the same Robison
brothers who ran the Spiders. Attendance was so bad at League
Park—a total of about six thousand fans for the season—the Spiders subcontracted out their home games to other cities. Their
home record therefore was just 9-32, their road record 11-102.

In 1901, Schmit became a pioneer of sorts. At age thirty-five,
he made four appearances, three of them as a starter, for the Baltimore Orioles in the inaugural season of the American League.
Somehow, despite an ERA of 1.99, he managed to go 0-2.

When he continued to barnstorm with local teams after his
retirement, Schmit gloried in his two nicknames, entertaining
fans with a thick German accent and theatrical ways. In 1906,
according to a *Detroit Free Press* article, Schmit was playing an
exhibition game in Joliet. The umpire announced beforehand,
"Ladies and gentlemen, the batteries for today will be Schmit
and Reading for Logan Square and Marshall and Rundle for
Joliet." Schmit, standing right behind the umpire, then stepped
up to announce, "Ladies and schentlemen, der umpire for der
game today will be Mister Miller of Joliet and he will, as usual,
slightly favor the home club mit his decisions."

JOSÉ LIMA, "WORST PITCHER ON EARTH"

José Lima had a flamboyant personality and a searing fastball
during two strong seasons. Somehow, he rode those assets to
a lucrative thirteen-year career in the majors that eventually
terminated in a record of 89-102 and an ERA of 5.26. His name
also became the eponym for two very different concepts: Lima
himself dubbed his pitching starts "Lima Time," a phrase that
quickly, laughingly caught on with fans and media. Less flat-
tering was a fantasy baseball term, the popular LIMA Plan,

invented by Ron Shandler, named after the pitcher, and a clever acronym for Low Investment Mound Aces. Shandler's strategy involved purchasing low-cost, flawed starting pitchers such as Lima with high strikeout-to-walk ratios, then using them for as few innings as allowed by a rotisserie league. Lima the actual red-blooded pitcher, however, was used for far too many innings, which was a big part of the problem.

Lima was once a hot Dominican prospect with uncharacteristic control for such a young starter. He really came into his own after he was traded from Detroit to Houston in 1996. At his best, Lima was truly a force on the mound. In 1998, he pitched 233⅓ innings and was 16-8 with a 3.70 ERA, a 5.28 strikeout-to-walk ratio that led the league, with a wins above replacement (WAR) of 3.5. The following season, he was even better. Lima finished fourth in the Cy Young voting after going 21-10, with a 3.58 ERA and a WAR of 4.3 in 246⅓ innings. His numbers only told part of the story. Lima was a babbler and fist pumper on the mound, a shameless, lovable self-promoter in the clubhouse, and a self-styled salsa musician. "He's one of the few pitchers who played his own music on the days that he pitched," his Houston teammate Lance Berkman said. "You knew every time he was pitching, because he had his own video up on the board." Lima would sign autographs for hours, asking kids, "What time is it?" The fans would yell back, "Lima Time!"

Then, mysteriously and swiftly, Lima lost his stuff and his clout. There was great debate over the cause of his demise. He might have thrown too many innings at the height of his success. He also didn't enjoy switching from the pitcher-friendly Astrodome to a new stadium in Houston. The closer fences messed with his mind and delivery. His statistical descent was startling. In 2000, he went 7-16 with a 6.65 ERA, yielding a franchise record forty-eight homers and a league-high 145 earned runs. Lima never really recovered his equilibrium. In June 2001, he was traded back to Detroit, where he earned as much as $7.25 million in 2002. When he was dropped by the Tigers, Lima uttered an all-time gem: "If I can't pitch on this team—the worst or second-worst team in baseball—where am I going to pitch? If I can't start on this ball club, I must be the worst pitcher on Earth."

He would not give up, though. Lima spent time in Newark, in the minors, before he was purchased by the Royals in 2003. The Dodgers and the Mets gave him a try, too. Los Angeles proved a comfortable, albeit brief, home stand. Lima appeared in the Dodger Stadium parking lot before one home game with his own salsa band, Banda Mambo, and was invited to sing the national anthem before another. He spoke happily then, to anyone who would listen, about becoming a professional singer after retirement. Lima also threw a shocking five-hit, complete-game shutout in 2004 against St. Louis in Game 3 of the National League Division Series. But then again, with the Royals in 2005 and the Mets in 2006—when the righty was 0-4 with an eye-popping 9.87 ERA—Lima Time became a target of derision more than anything, particularly in impatient New York.

This fall from grace didn't seem to bother Lima much. He showed up at spring training for the Mets in Port St. Lucie wearing a silver three-piece suit with a black fedora and an assortment of bling. "I've never worn the same one twice," he said, boasting of two thousand suits. "I give the old ones to my brothers. They wear the same size I do." He asked the Mets if he and his band could perform before a game. Lima loved the sport and the limelight so much he kept pitching in the Dominican winter league, then in Korea, and then in 2009 for Edmonton of the Golden Baseball League, where a fan club sprouted for him yet again. He was still losing, though, with a 1-2 record and another defeat in the playoffs. Lima might still be out there trying, if he hadn't died of a heart attack in 2010 at the age of thirty-seven. His passing was mourned by fans of baseball and salsa alike.

DICKIE NOLES, ONE-MAN TRANSACTION

Dickie Noles was signed, traded, released, and re-signed so often—eight times in eleven seasons—you could excuse the poor fellow if he didn't quite know where he was pitching on any particular night. But what made Noles's mediocre career fairly unique, besides the embarrassing way it ended, was that Noles was once traded for himself. Even considering the sometimes random maneuverings of general managers, this was a special occasion. On September 22, 1987, Noles was dealt by the Cubs to the Tigers for a player to be named later. Then, on October 23, after he'd blown two of four save opportunities for Detroit with a 4.50 ERA, he became that player to be named later and was returned to the Cubs. This came perilously close to a loan arrangement, like the ones that soccer teams employ in Europe. The office of Commissioner Peter Ueberroth investigated the deal, but Detroit's general manager, Bill Lajoie, insisted it was not a case of collusion and that the two clubs simply couldn't agree on other players to complete a bigger deal.

"Whoever made the complaint did not consider that this could be a forerunner or the first part of a major transaction," Lajoie said. "There were several other players mentioned originally. I'm surprised it even came up."

The Tigers, under the manager Sparky Anderson, were on their way to winning a division title that season, though Noles would not be invited onto the postseason roster. The pitcher found the whole situation patently absurd.

"Sparky Anderson had said once that the only reason Dickie Noles was in the big leagues is because he throws at people," Noles said in an interview with *The New York Times.* "Then I go there on Sept. 22, we're playing the Red Sox at Fenway Park, and he brings me in in the ninth inning to get the save. I had a funny feeling I was going to be that player [to be named later]. I knew when the trade was made that there was no agreement on the player, and I knew [Cubs GM] Dallas Green was going to try to pull a pretty good arm out of it. The Tigers just weren't going to do it, and I know how Dallas is. I'm sure he said, 'Well, just give him back,' and they gave me back."

Anderson began to sour on Noles when he came in from the bullpen on September 26 with the bases loaded, hoping to protect a two-run lead against the Blue Jays, and immediately gave up a three-run walk-off triple to Jesse Barfield. Even after he was bundled back to Chicago like so much damaged merchandise, Noles never pitched again for the Cubs. He had brief, humiliating stints with Baltimore in 1988 and with the Phillies in 1990—not to be confused with longer, embarrassing seasons in 1984, 1985, and 1986, when he finished with ERAs over 5.00 for three different teams. In 1988, Noles made two appearances for the Orioles, losing both games. He gave up six hits and six runs against the Tigers in just two innings and yielded four runs on five hits in one and one-third innings against the Red Sox. His ERA for 1988 was 24.30. Then, on May 8, 1990, he made his last major-league appearance with the Phillies, his only game of the year. He entered in the tenth inning of a 2–2 game, got one out, then gave up a single and the game-winning walk-off double to Rafael Ramirez. That left Noles with an ERA of 27.00 for 1990. And that was enough for everyone.

ANTHONY YOUNG, HISTORIC LOSER

Forget sabermetrics for a moment. Sometimes you just have to judge a pitcher on that purest, simplest of stats: Did he win the game, or did he lose? This is not always a fair measure of a man, but then baseball is a zero-sum sport in which the ultimate goal is to hold the opponents to fewer runs over nine (or a few extra) innings. And by this particular standard, Anthony Young must gain entry into any book of failure.

From May 1992 to July 1993, Young became the showcase for the Mets' futility in New York—as if that club required such a living symbol—by dropping twenty-seven consecutive decisions and smashing the all-time record. In truth, Young wasn't terrible. He was merely bad. There were pitchers in the league, and on the Mets, with a worse ERA than his 4.36 mark during this particular span. The fact that the managers Jeff Torborg and Dallas Green kept throwing Young out on the mound for his turn in the rotation, again and again, was a reminder that Mets pitchers had a grand tradition of gaudy losing, like when Roger Craig dropped twenty-four and twenty-two games in 1962 and 1963.

During Young's streak, New York fans were remarkably and uncharacteristically patient; the Mets went 59-103 in 1993, after all, so there were other problems with the team besides Young. He would receive much advice from self-proclaimed pitching experts and psychics. Young was sent good-luck charms. He was invited on air with Jay Leno and met with the surviving family of Cliff Curtis, the pitcher who had set the consecutive-loss record back in 1910–1911.

The streak was a great gift to modern-day record keepers, who dissected it by all computer models available. Young was 0-19 in night games, for example, and 0-8 in day games. He was 0-14 as a starter and 0-13 as a reliever. He had particularly bad luck coming out of the bullpen, clearly deserving better. When the closer John Franco was out with an injury, Young converted twelve straight save opportunities and amassed twenty-three and two-thirds straight scoreless innings. He never earned a victory during that span, because he never blew a lead, which would have been a requisite.

"I got a bad rap on that," Young told the New York *Daily*

News. "I always said I didn't feel like I was pitching badly. It just happened to happen to me. I don't feel like I deserve it, but I'm known for it. It was an 82-year-old record and it might be 82 more years before it's broken. Everything that could happen, happened. It was just destiny, I guess."

The streak was finally broken on July 28, 1993, when Young was brought in to protect another one-run lead in the top of the ninth inning. The Florida Marlins scored to tie the game on a throwing error by Todd Hundley, and then the Mets won the game in the bottom of the inning on a walk-off double by Eddie Murray. Young was mobbed on the mound by teammates and coaches. The crowd at Shea Stadium gave him a standing ova- tion, bigger than the one for Murray. "Thankfully, it's over with," Young said at the time. "Maybe now I'll start a winning streak."

It was not to be, however. After two successful saves, Young was called into a game on August 13 to protect a 5–4 lead in Phil- adelphia, with one on and two out in the bottom of the ninth. Familiar disaster resulted—a walk, a throwing error by the Mets' shortstop, Kevin Baez, that tied the game, an intentional walk, and then a grand-slam walk-off homer by Kim Batiste for four unearned runs and a 9–5 loss, Young's fourteenth defeat of the season. Young was traded to the Cubs, then hooked on with the Astros in 1996. His final record was 15-48, despite a very decent 3.89 ERA and a positive WAR (wins above replacement) of 1.4 over his six seasons. In other words, an average pitcher in Young's situation might have been expected to lose even more games.

Young made the best of things, considering. He earned more than $1.2 million in the major leagues and continued to pitch in the minors through 1998. After retirement, he participated in Mets fantasy camps, appeared at memorabilia shows, and coached kids who were sharp enough to research their instruc- tor on the Internet. "Once they find out you were in the big leagues, they 'Google' you," Young said. "Then they say, 'Coach, you're known for a losing streak!'"

BOTTOM TEN

1 **HERM WEHMEIER** — Couldn't find control until it was too late.

2 **TODD VAN POPPEL** — A fastball wasn't enough.

3 **CRAZY SCHMIT** — Worst pitcher on the worst team in baseball.

4 **JOSÉ LIMA** — Much more image than substance.

5 **LES SWEETLAND** — Had a 6.10 ERA and walked 358 batters over 740⅔ innings from 1927 to 1931.

6 **JARET WRIGHT** — Earned more than $30 million, somehow, with a career ERA of 5.09.

7 **JAIME NAVARRO** — During three workhorse seasons with the White Sox from 1997 to 1999, he had a 6.06 ERA and threw forty-two wild pitches.

8 **DICKIE NOLES** — On both ends of a trade.

9 **KYLE DAVIES** — In 2011, he was 1-9 with a 6.75 ERA for the Royals.

10 **ANTHONY YOUNG** — Remarkably consistent loser.

4 $23,000,097 PER WIN
Most Overpaid Yankees

THE FOOLISH, RASH overpayment of undertalented players is a modern-era phenomenon, born from free agency and George Steinbrenner's checkbook. There is no shortage of such examples, but don't expect to see any names here dating before 1974. Back then, wads of money were not being thrown at anybody, regardless of merit. Now, of course, the economics of all professional sports has gone completely haywire. Players enter contract years knowing full well they may strike it rich with one well-timed season. Occasionally, a coveted free agent will sign a long-term deal with a big-market team that works out for everyone. More often, these pacts are regretted by general managers just four or five months after the ink dries. Soon, high-priced starters are demoted to middle-relief work and aging, creaky third basemen—that would be you, Alex Rodríguez—are slowly transitioned to designated hitter. One hard-and-fast rule stands in these matters: nobody admits publicly to a mistake until the next general manager takes charge.

There are so many of these costly miscalculations over the past four decades they must be divided here into two categories: overpaid by the Yankees, and overpaid by everyone else. As always, Yankees first.

KEI IGAWA AND HIS $46,000,194 PRICE TAG

The Yanks have thrown money at a lot of players, many of them unworthy of such bonanzas. And in the first decade of the twenty-first century, the overly optimistic evaluations of free-agent pitchers were legion, from Jaret Wright to A. J. Burnett. But when it came to scouting and investment gaffes, the lefty starter Kei Igawa always stood far above the rest. Igawa was a superstar in Japan, averaging fifteen victories over his last five years with the Hanshin Tigers while leading the Japan Central League in strikeouts during three of those seasons. But there was already considerable evidence—the Yanks should have learned this lesson from their experience with Hideki Irabu—that pitching well in Japan doesn't necessarily translate into pitching well in the majors.

In November 2006, the Hanshin Tigers "posted" Igawa, the process by which Nippon Professional Baseball organized an international auction. The Yanks were hungry for starters at the time, particularly left-handers, and the club's Far East scouts were telling Brian Cashman that Igawa was the real deal. The Yanks had just lost a bidding war for another Japanese starter, Daisuke Matsuzaka, signed by the archrival Red Sox to an outrageous six-year, $52 million pact, in addition to a $51.1 million payment to the Seibu Lions. The Yanks paid Hanshin $26,000,194 (those last three numbers were Igawa's strikeout total in 2006) merely for the rights to negotiate with Igawa. They then signed Igawa for $20 million over five seasons, increasing their disastrous investment to just over $46 million.

During a big press gathering for Igawa in January 2007, extraordinary things were promised by all. Before the season

Kei Igawa signed with the Yankees in 2006, back when everybody
was still happy about it. *AP Photo/Kathy Willens*

began, Igawa blogged for his fans, "I feel a burden of anxiety
at the opening of my first season in the Majors but it is over-
whelmed by the excitement of being a home player standing on
the field at Yankee Stadium. I will strive to do my best at all
times."

Igawa strived. He never thrived, however. He was a hard-
working, sincere, and modest athlete. But he was also, sadly, a
terrible failure from day one. In his very first start on April 7 at
Yankee Stadium against the Orioles, he allowed seven earned
runs in five innings. Within weeks, despite some kind, public words of encouragement, Cashman and manager Joe Torre
understood they had a real problem on their hands. By May 7,
they sent Igawa to Tampa to work on his mechanics in the minors
with the coaches Nardi Contreras and Billy Connors, two fix-it

guys who rarely succeeded in repairing much of anything. The coaches completely reinvented Igawa's delivery, from arm angle to leg push-off. They even had him change foot positions on the pitching rubber. None of it really worked. His location was up in the strike zone way too often, and he didn't have the stuff to make up for that. Igawa went back and forth between the Yanks and their minor-league teams for two seasons. His final appearance in the majors came on June 27, 2008, when he gave up two hits in one inning of no-sweat, mop-up relief, successfully protecting a nine-run lead. He finished with a 2-4 record in sixteen games in his major-league career, with a humiliating ERA of 6.66. The Yankees had paid about $2.88 million for each of his appearances in pinstripes—or $23,000,097 per win.

There is an upbeat coda of sorts to this story. Igawa never regained the form he once showed in Japan, yet he soldiered on in the minors, fulfilling his contractual obligations honorably in the minor-league outposts of Trenton and Scranton. He never complained, despite injuries, and he counseled many younger pitchers who would soon surpass him on the organizational depth chart. Occasionally, Japanese tourists would come and greet Igawa in minor-league parks, wishing him well. Igawa was always gracious. He might have been an embarrassment to the Yankees' scouting system and to Cashman. Never to Japan.

CARL PAVANO, YANKEE KILLER

Carl Pavano has really experienced several different pitching careers in the majors. He floundered early with the Expos, then became a star and a bargain for the Marlins. Much later, he was a respectable starter for the Twins. But there was also a four-season stint with the Yankees, from 2005 to 2008, that stands out as something of a burlesque show and one of the worst deals ever made by Brian Cashman.

In fairness, the media and most experts were largely supportive of the transaction when it first came down. Pavano was coming off an 18-8 season, with a 3.00 ERA and 222⅓ innings pitched.
He was not only an ace in waiting; he was an iron man. He'd performed well under pressure,
too. During the 2003 World
Series, Pavano logged nine
innings against the Yanks
and gave up only one earned
run. His eight-inning start
in Game 4, which ended in
a Florida victory, was arguably the pivotal performance
that sank the Bombers. So
a $38 million contract over
four years to such a conquer-
ing foe did not seem at all
extravagant, particularly by
Yankees standards.

Pavano's misadventures in
pinstripes, however, quickly
became downright mythic.
After a respectable start, he
injured his right shoulder
and headed for what would

Yet another injury for Carl Pavano,
as he's escorted off the mound by
a Yankee trainer. *AP Photo/Kathy
Willens*

become his second home with the Yankees, the disabled list. He
suffered a bruised buttocks—the butt of many jokes—during
spring training in 2006 and headed for the DL. He was still
recovering from this odd, humiliating ailment in August, making rehab starts in Florida, when he fractured two ribs ramming
his Porsche into an eighteen-wheel semi in West Palm Beach,
with the swimsuit model Gia Allemand as his passenger. Pavano
didn't bother telling the Yanks about any of this for some eleven
days, at which time the team was expecting him to finally come

off the disabled list. There were many rumors to the effect that Pavano was, umm . . . distracted by Allemand at the time of the accident. The New York *Daily News* reported the incident with the headline "Crash Yank's Hottie." But in 2007, Allemand told *Steppin' Out* magazine, "The whole thing was definitely blown out of proportion. People thought we were doing stuff and that's what caused the car accident, but it was eleven in the morning. We just finished eating breakfast. Trust me, we weren't doing anything except driving." Driving badly, she might have added. Pavano didn't pitch at all in 2006. As he prepared to start Opening Day in April 2007, Allemand reportedly dumped him right before game time. "Carl and I are enemies," she told Chaunce Hayden, in another *Steppin' Out* piece. Pavano was hammered that day for five runs (four earned) in four and one-third innings.

This was all getting a bit much for everyone in New York, including manager Joe Torre and Pavano's teammates. The pitcher hadn't really maintained contact with the Yankees players during his rehab stints, even when the club was playing in Tampa. Steady Mike Mussina was the first to go on the record grumping about Pavano's many problems. "It didn't look good from a player's and teammate's standpoint," Mussina said. "Was everything a coincidence? Over and over again? I don't know."

The calamities just didn't stop. Pavano suffered an elbow strain and was placed on the fifteen-day DL, yet again, on April 15, 2007. By May, he had decided to undergo Tommy John surgery to reconstruct his pitching elbow. That was it for another season, and by then Pavano was more or less viewed as a lost cause by Cashman, the man who signed him. That winter, the general manager asked Pavano to restructure his contract, without losing money, so he could be moved to the minors and clear space for somebody else on the forty-man roster. This might have been an appropriate moment for Pavano to make a goodwill gesture toward his employers. His new agent, Tom O'Connell, refused. By the time Pavano appeared in his first rehab start with the Charleston RiverDogs on July 29, 2008, his infamous contract was nearing its expiration date. He made seven starts with New York that season and finished with a 5.77 ERA. At least Yankees fans got their closure, a few last chances to boo the guy. Following a visit from Torre and the trainer to the mound in the sixth inning of a game on September 14, Pavano limped to the dugout and was inundated with jeers from the capacity crowd at Yankee Stadium. His final appearance in pinstripes on September 25 was appropriate enough: Pavano gave up five runs on eight hits in three and two-thirds innings. During his four years in the Bronx, Pavano had managed only a record of 9-8 in twenty-six games. He pitched a total of 145⅔ innings, never posting an ERA under 4.76 in any of those abbreviated seasons. The Yankees had paid him nearly $261,000 for every inning pitched, or about $4 million per injury.

JASON GIAMBI AND THE ART OF EXCESS

When the Yankees captured a World Series title in 1996, beginning a six-year run of dynastic proportion, their player payroll stood at $61.5 million. And while they still led the majors in spending, it was not by much at all. Position players were mostly either homegrown talent, such as Bernie Williams and Derek Jeter, or trade acquisitions, like Tino Martinez and Paul O'Neill. This roster had remarkable chemistry and might well become known as the last club ever to navigate so many rounds of playoffs in order to capture five league pennants and four championships over six seasons.

At the close of 2001, however, several core players retired or played out their contracts. Tino Martinez, their free-agent first baseman, an outstanding fielder, was coming off a thirty-four-homer, 113-RBI season but was turning thirty-four over the winter, and the Yankees decided to look elsewhere. Unfortunately, they looked to Oakland, where Jason Giambi was three years younger and coming off a near-MVP season with a .342 batting average, thirty-eight homers, and 120 RBIs. The Yanks signed Giambi to a seven-year, $120 million deal, which smacked of unnecessary excess for a number of reasons. For one thing, they could have signed the popular Martinez to a far more modest pact, one similar to the two-year, $13 million contract he inked with St. Louis. This was also just three short months after the 9/11 terrorist attacks in New York City. The city's economy was imploding, and nobody was in the mood for such showmanship.

Giambi, through no fault of his own, thus became a symbol of corporate gluttony and the end of a Yankee dynasty. In Oakland, he had been known as a free spirit in a lighthearted clubhouse. As a Yankee, he immediately sacrificed that identity, adhering to team rules by shaving his goatee and cutting his scraggly hair. And while his impressive bat speed and power numbers remained intact for several years, his batting averages swooned to .250 in 2003 and .208 in 2004.

His declining offense wasn't the whole story, though. Giambi became creakier after suffering a series of injuries, including a severe tear to tissue in his foot. He wasn't a great first baseman to begin with and slowly became lousier. He was often used instead as a designated hitter. Then, compounding buyer's regret, he brought scandal with him to the Bronx, far worse than facial hair. Giambi became a big part of the BALCO steroid probe on the West Coast after involving himself with performance-enhancing drugs shortly after signing with the Yanks. He described to a grand jury, in explicit fashion, how he injected himself with human growth hormone during 2003 after already experimenting with steroids in 2001. His testimony was illegally leaked to the public, forcing Giambi to issue a vague apology to fans during a 2005 press conference. This only increased demands for the player to explain himself more specifically, creating an unpleasant distraction around a Yankees team that was no longer capturing any championships. In 2007, Giambi came close to a full confession of steroid use when he told *USA Today*, "I was wrong for using that stuff. What we should have done a long time ago was stand up—players, ownership, everybody—and said, 'We made a mistake.'" He still wouldn't give many details, until the 2011 perjury trial of Barry Bonds. Then Giambi told a jury in San Francisco that he became more deeply involved with steroids during a tour of Japan by Major League Baseball. Barry Bonds had brought his trainer, Greg Anderson, along for the trip. "I was picking Greg's brain about what kind of training Barry was doing," Giambi said. "I mean, he was an incredible baseball player, and I just wanted to continue my career." Giambi said he purchased drugs from Anderson and used them until he suffered an injury in 2003.

During Giambi's seven years with the Yankees, he hit 209 homers—or very nearly 30 per season—and drove in 604 RBIs. From a statistical standpoint, this signing was satisfactory. Yet Giambi's arrival, in many eyes, was the very moment when the Yanks jumped the shark. By 2007, the team's streak of nine straight American League East titles was broken while the club's payroll stood at a gaudy $218.3 million, an increase of more than 350 percent from the pre-Giambi era. In 2008, Giambi's final season in New York, the Yanks failed to make the playoffs for the first time since the 1994 baseball strike. Some of this was due to the roster's natural aging process and inflationary factors. It should be noted also that many of the Yanks' starting pitchers back in their salad days of the late 1990s were mercenary free agents. Giambi, however, will always be remembered in the Bronx for his grandiose contract, his shoddy defense, his deteriorating stats, and his drug scandal. His predecessors at first base, Don Mattingly and Tino Martinez, were beloved. Giambi was merely tolerated.

ED WHITSON, BITTEN BY THE BIG APPLE

In the Bronx, the name Ed Whitson long ago became shorthand for "a guy who can't handle New York." Talented free agents from smaller markets were regularly passed over by the Yanks for fear they had too much Ed Whitson in their DNA. In 2010, desperately short in his rotation, the general manager, Brian Cashman, still wouldn't trade for Zack Greinke, because he dreaded the potential Whitson factor.

Whitson himself became a free agent after the 1984 season, after he went 14-8 with a 3.24 ERA for the San Diego Padres. He was a promising starter, but he joined the Bombers at the height of their madness under an unraveling Billy Martin. If only he'd begun his tenure with some success, well, maybe Whitson would have survived. But after signing his five-year, $4.4 million contract—a major investment, for the time—Whitson immediately floundered in his Yankee debut at Fenway and went 1-6 with a 6.23 ERA over his first eleven starts. The fans jeered him mercilessly, waiting outside the ballpark sometimes to have at him. Hate mail arrived by the bundle at his locker, and it became clear that Whitson was not one of those guys who could shrug off harsh criticism by crowds or columnists. He stopped wearing his Yankees cap anywhere outside the clubhouse. Whitson would claim somebody placed nails under his car in his driveway at home. He banned his wife, Kathleen, from ever coming to Yankee Stadium, fearing for her life.

He briefly turned things around in mid-season of 1985, going 9-1 with a 2.27 ERA over sixteen starts. But then Whitson faltered during a key game against the Blue Jays in September, spurring a Yankee meltdown, and Martin completely gave up on him. To the manager, Whitson became known only as "Whatchamacallit" and was treated as a nonperson. After Whitson was pulled from his next start, the two men became involved in a Baltimore hotel lounge brawl on September 22 that injured both participants. The scrappy Martin, giving up forty pounds and four inches in reach, suffered a broken arm, while one of Whitson's ribs was cracked. Details of that fight were reported in several publications, including *Sports Illustrated:*

At approximately 12:20 a.m. Martin was sitting in the Cross Keys lounge with Dale Berra and Berra's wife, Leigh. Martin and Berra were told that Whitson was having words with another patron, and they rushed to his aid. But when Martin got there, he claims Whitson turned on him, and suddenly they had their hands on each other. They tumbled to the floor and had to be separated by various Yankee personnel. Whitson later said Martin had "sucker-punched" him, a charge Martin denied. "That guy's crazy," said Martin. "I just tried to help him. What's the matter with him? Can't he hold his liquor?" Whitson, still under restraint, kept screaming at Martin, and Martin, never one to turn away from a good fight, kept advancing as Whitson was being pushed outside. As they neared the door, Whitson made a charge and, arms pinned back, kicked Martin in the groin. Martin, who was doubled over in pain, screamed, "O.K., now I'm going to kill you. Now you did it." Again the two were separated, and Whitson was taken outside. Martin followed. Whitson rushed Martin and the two went crashing to the pavement. They flailed away until pulled apart. Whitson shouted at his skipper, "You've tried to bury me here; you're trying to ruin me."

Later, at Memorial Stadium, Martin, his arm in a sling, said, "I didn't win. I can't fight feet. Maybe I ought to go to one of those karate schools."

Martin was fired at the end of the season, in part because of this altercation. His replacement, Lou Piniella, attempted a different strategy in 1986 with Whitson. The pitcher would start games on the road but appear only in relief at Yankee Stadium. This did not work that well, either. Over less than two seasons, Whitson was 15-10 but had a 5.38 ERA when the Yankees decided to cut their losses and deal him back to San Diego on July 9 for Tim Stoddard. Years later, Whitson told ESPN of his frustrations with New Yorkers. "It's like working in an office and your boss comes in and says, 'You suck,' after you've tried your best," Whitson said. "Now multiply that by 50,000 bosses, all of them telling you that you suck, and imagine what that feels like. You feel like everybody's against you, and sometimes you just want to quit. But you can't ever quit."

Once returned to the welcoming bosom of San Diego, Whitson became effective again. He had two particularly fine seasons in 1989 and 1990, when he went a combined 30-20 with an ERA of 2.63. Whitson had combined ERAs under 3.80 in San Diego, San Francisco, Pittsburgh, and Cleveland. Just not in a city of eight million critics.

JAVY VÁZQUEZ, DOUBLE DIPPING

In the middle of the first decade of the twenty-first century, when the Yankees were desperate to rekindle their mojo and reestablish a dynasty, they overpaid many high-profile starters—Randy Johnson (a disappointment) and Kevin Brown (a disaster) among them. But Javier Vázquez stood out if only because the Yanks failed to learn any lessons from his first visit to New York and reacquired him nearly five years later for a similar, exorbitant price tag and with the same sad results.

Vázquez seemed to have his head screwed on right and always said the correct things about pitching in New York. He

Javier Vázquez gives up the killer grand-slam homer to Johnny Damon with his very first pitch in Game 7 of the 2004 American League Championship Series. There were many bad pitches to come. *AP Photo/Bill Kostroun*

denied that the pressure or criticism bothered him, yet it must have been extremely difficult dealing with the trauma of October 20, 2004, when he entered Game 7 of the American League Championship Series in the second inning against the Red Sox and gave up a first-pitch grand slam to Johnny Damon. The Yanks had acquired Vázquez before the 2004 season in a trade with the Montreal Expos and then signed him to a four-year, $45 million contract. "I want to be a Yankee for more than a year," Vázquez said. One year was all that could be tolerated. The Yanks paid him $9 million in 2004 to post a 4.91 ERA during the regular season. Then, in the playoffs, he was tagged for five runs in five innings by the Twins and seven runs in six and one-third innings by the Red Sox. The Yanks immediately dealt him in a multiplayer trade to Arizona for Randy Johnson, and everyone figured that would be that.

In December 2009, Brian Cashman was desperate again to extend his rotation and believed that Vázquez still had enough stuff to thrive in the Bronx. The pitcher was coming off a 15-10 season in Atlanta, with a 2.87 ERA. In theory, enough time had passed since the Red Sox meltdown. The Yanks ignored his history of playoff chokes in the Bronx and with the White Sox, overlooked his track record of failure in the American League, and agreed to pick up his $11.5 million salary for one season. Yet again, nothing went right.

Vázquez still sounded sane and determined, even as his ERA climbed to 9.78 in May. "I'm just making terrible pitches," he insisted. "You can make them in the American League or the National League. You can make them anywhere. If you listen to what everybody says, you're gonna get crazy." Perhaps his problems were not psychological but simply the result of a fastball that was no longer fast. He struggled to reach the mid-eighties on the radar gun, which was only good enough to produce a record of 10-10 with a 5.32 ERA. Vázquez was demoted to the bullpen and kept off the postseason roster. Twice burned, the Yanks did not re-sign him after the season, and Vázquez somehow landed at age thirty-four one more lucrative, $7 million pact with the Marlins. He fared a little better in Florida than in New York, but then again Vázquez always did better outside New York. His cumulative stats over two stints and two seasons with the Yankees: 24-20 with a 5.09 ERA, not counting his playoff meltdowns. For these performances, Cashman had laid out $20.5 million, or nearly $1 million per victory.

KEVIN BROWN, HITTING THE WALL

If only Kevin Brown hadn't been quite so surly, perhaps management, fans, and media in New York might have forgiven at least a few of his many trespasses on the mound. As it was, the Georgian's fish-out-of-water stay in the Bronx was uniquely expensive and unpleasant.

Back in 1998, Brown had signed the first $100 million–plus contract in baseball, agreeing to a seven-year, $105 million deal with the Los Angeles Dodgers. While Brown had posted many lights-out seasons in his career with his sinking fastball, he was already thirty-three years old at the time, which meant the contract would endure past his fortieth birthday. While the Dodgers' investment appeared overgenerous, the Yankees came out looking far worse when they traded for Brown and the final two years on his contract in December 2003. The Dodgers had managed to squeeze two or three decent seasons out of Brown before the Yankees went on the hook for $31.4 million with the fading, nasty-tempered thirty-eight-year-old starter. At the time, the Dodgers also were rightly suspicious that Brown had been involved with performance-enhancing drugs, possibly contributing to his mood swings and health problems. *The Mitchell Report* later detailed allegations by Kirk Radomski, the Mets' clubhouse employee, that he sold both human growth hormone and nandrolone, a steroid, to Brown while he was pitching in Los Angeles.

The Yanks got exactly what they deserved for such foolishness. Brown was 14-13 with an ERA of 4.95 over his two seasons in the Bronx. His tenure there was marked by sharp exchanges with reporters, on those occasions he deigned to speak with them at all. Brown also grew increasingly isolated from teammates, losing their faith altogether on September 3, 2004, when he punched a clubhouse wall during a losing start against the

Orioles. The blow fractured his left hand. Brown missed more than three weeks recovering from necessary surgery during a tight pennant race with Boston. "Stupidity," Brown said. "I reacted to frustration I'd swallowed all year. There are no excuses. I let it boil over and I did something stupid. I owe my teammates an apology for letting my emotions take over like that." Those teammates just shook their heads at such an antic. "To physically do something to injure yourself? I can't relate to that," Mike Mussina said. When Brown finally returned, the Yanks wished he hadn't. He was handed the ball to start Game 7 of the 2004 American League Championship Series against the Red Sox, arguably one of the three or four most important moments in Yankees history. He gave up four hits, two walks, a homer to David Ortiz, and five earned runs in one and one-third innings.

By the time his contract expired in 2005, not a soul in New York wanted to bring back Brown. He retired soon after with 211 victories, six All-Star appearances, a ton of money, and ill feelings about pinstripes.

HIDEKI IRABU, LOST IN TRANSLATION

Hideki Irabu was always a man torn sadly in several different directions, desperate to make it big in America. He never quite succeeded at anything except angering his boss, George Steinbrenner, who once labeled Irabu a "fat pus-sy toad."

Hideki was born in Hirara, Okinawa; his mother was a native Okinawan, and his biological father was an American serviceman who would not be part of Hideki's life. Instead, the boy was raised by his mom and a Japanese stepfather, Ichiro Irabu, a restaurateur in Amagasaki and the common-law husband to Hideki's mom. Hideki faced all the prejudices growing up that traditionally met foreign-born kids in largely homogeneous Japan. He would sometimes get into fights with other children who called him *ainoko*, or "half-breed." He was drafted at age seventeen and began playing in 1987 for the Lotte Orions, who later became the Chiba Lotte Marines, in the Pacific League. He was a six-foot, four-inch giant who owned a wicked ninety-eight-mile-per-hour fastball, and he led the league in strikeouts and ERA in 1995. Irabu was so good over the course of nine seasons in Japan he was given the nickname Kurage, or "Jellyfish," because a manager commented that Irabu had stung his team like a *kurage*. Irabu soon started hankering to play in the United States, the ultimate challenge, but this was not done very often back then, and Chiba resisted his requests. Eventually, in January 1997, his negotiating rights were sold to the San Diego Padres. Irabu didn't want to play for the Padres, despite an offer of more than $4 million over three years. He demanded a bigger stage and fancied himself a Yankee—Irabu said he liked the team's colors. He forced a deal, signing a four-year contract in the Bronx for $12.8 million.

In some photographs, from some angles, he bore a striking resemblance to Babe Ruth himself. Irabu pitched in several minor-league games and greatly impressed Steinbrenner by asking his manager in Tampa whether he should drill an opponent with a fastball following a bench-clearing brawl. On July 10, 1997, Irabu made his debut with the Yankees against the Tigers before a crowd of 51,901 curious fans, some three hundred reporters, and a television audience back in Japan estimated at 35 million. Japanese players in the major leagues were still very much a novelty. Irabu, a large man of few words, oozed both mystery and charisma. After being honored earlier in the day with a ceremony at city hall with Mayor Rudy Giuliani, Irabu performed wonderfully in this pressure cooker, striking out nine and yielding just five hits and two runs in a six-and-two-third-inning start for a 10–3 Yankee victory.

Unfortunately, that day proved to be the high point of Irabu's career in America. He was hammered by Cleveland, Milwaukee, and Seattle in his next three starts. Before the year was done, Irabu was sent down to the minors for a spell and finished his first major-league season with a 7.09 ERA. The following season, 1998, was more hopeful, as he posted a 13-9 mark with a 4.06 ERA. In spring training camp, he met his biological father for the first time, conversing through an interpreter. "He did not want anything from me except to know me and my kids," Irabu said. "He never asked for anything."

Irabu failed to cover first base during a 1999 spring training game played under the nose of Steinbrenner, who immediately dubbed him a fat pus-sy toad, which was not to be confused with a jellyfish. He was almost respectable in 1999, another world championship year for the Yankees, and threw a few rocky innings against the Red Sox in one American League Championship Series game. By this time, however, it was obvious Irabu would never meet the oversized expectations that burdened him. He'd sit alone at his locker, magnets attached to his body in the hopes of restoring his cosmic energy. He became the one consistently depressing clubhouse sight during these glory years for the Yankees. Irabu was overweight and overwrought. The Yanks dealt him to Montreal at the end of the 1999 season in a trade for a more effective pitcher, Ted Lilly, among others. Irabu was a failure with the Expos and later the Rangers, returning to Japan a defeated man yet still ever hopeful of reigniting his career. He pitched for the Hanshin Tigers in 2003 with some success, then came back to the States to play for the Long Beach Armada of the independent Golden Baseball League and to become a part owner in several Japanese restaurants around Los Angeles. He dabbled in some youth baseball coaching. On the surface, it seemed, he had built himself a steady existence with a wife and two children. He was not at peace, however, and was found dead in his Rancho Palos Verdes home in July 2011, an apparent victim of suicide. There was no note left behind, no further clues to the inner life of this erstwhile Japanese icon.

BOTTOM TEN

1   **KEI IGAWA**   What were those scouts watching?

2   **CARL PAVANO**   He had the nerve to get better again in Minnesota.

3   **JASON GIAMBI**   Brought both shame and creakiness to the Bronx.

4   **ED WHITSON**   More than a little bit nervous in New York.

5   **JAVY VÁZQUEZ**   Fool me once, shame on you . . .

6   **KEVIN BROWN**   Never met a wall he didn't want to punch.

7   **HIDEKI IRABU**   Forever George Steinbrenner's "fat pus-sy toad."

8   **JARET WRIGHT**   So bad, the Yanks traded him with cash to Baltimore for the pitcher Chris Britton, who never won a game.

9   **ROGER CLEMENS (second time)**   Yanks went into orbit with the Rocket once too often in 2007.

10   **A. J. BURNETT**   Cashman gave Pittsburgh a $20 million rebate on the final two years of Burnett's bloated contract, and then the pitcher started winning games for the Pirates.

5 | TOO FAT TO BAT
Most Overpaid, Outside the Bronx

GEORGE STEINBRENNER WASN'T the only one with deep, stupid pockets. Consider:

BARRY ZITO AND THE SEVEN-YEAR STENCH

Back on December 29, 2006, the contract made considerable sense for the San Francisco Giants. Barry Zito was in his prime at twenty-eight years old, a former Cy Young winner, a three-time All-Star, a left-hander coming off yet another fine season for the Oakland A's (16-10, 3.83 ERA). He was also known as the biggest workhorse in the game. Zito, remarkably, had never missed a scheduled start. He started 208 games in the previous six seasons, throwing 213 innings or more in each of those years and leading the league in starts during four of them. He'd pitched well in the postseason, proving his mettle. He'd played in the Bay Area, so there would be no geographical adjustment necessary. Zito's fastball was only clocked in the high eighties, but nobody had a sharper, drop-off-the-table curveball. "You may as well not even look for it," Alex Rodríguez once said of Zito's curve, "because you're not going to hit it." Most of all, Zito was a perfect fit for the citizenry and fans of San Francisco, a freethinker whose mom was an ordained minister and father a classically trained musician. Zito was into positive vision. He liked stuffed animals and admired the look of the number 75 on his uniform, because the 7 appeared to cradle his name on the back of his jersey.

Zito was a little flaky, sure—some teammates called him Planet Zito—but people just shook their heads and said he was a lefty. So the Giants outbid the Mets, who would only guarantee five seasons, and made a super-deal with his super-agent, Scott Boras. They opened the vault for seven years and $126 million, plus an $18 million team option for 2014 with a $7 million buyout. The Giants were on the hook for at least $133 million, representing the biggest contract for any pitcher in major-league history. The owner Pete Magowan called it "the most important signing we've had since we first signed Barry Bonds." At his introductory press conference, Zito joked that he was going to reinvent himself. "I'm just thinking of canning the curveball. Other than that, nothing major," he said. Zito declared this was his place and time and promised not to put too much pressure on himself. "When you try to become some superhuman cartoon character," he said, "that's when things go wrong."

And then everything went wrong. Zito struggled from the start with the switch in leagues and, despite his vow to remain rooted in reality, was overwrought about expectations that came with the megadeal. "I've been trying to have a good game," he said after another bad start. "You can't try to do anything about it. You either do or you don't. I tried to get too fine with my pitches. I wasn't aggressive." His ERA ballooned to 4.53 in 2007 and to 5.15 in 2008. Very quickly, Zito was no longer considered one of baseball's elite pitchers. He changed his mechanics with some success, going to a three-quarters delivery in 2009 and relying more on a slider. Yet when the Giants advanced to the World Series in 2010, he was left off the postseason roster.

Then, in 2011, Zito made his first-ever trip to the disabled list, after injuring his right foot on a fielding play. He was demoted to spot starter upon his return and pitched just fifty-three and two-thirds innings that season.

Through his first five seasons with the Giants, Zito was 43-61 with a 4.55 ERA. He recovered his equilibrium somewhat in 2012, but the only question that remained, really, was whether the Giants could find any general manager to take Zito off their hands and pay just a fraction of his remaining contract. Zito did perform well during the 2012 postseason, when he pitched masterfully against the Cardinals in Game Five of the NLCS and beat Justin Verlander in Game 1 of the World Series, but two games does not $133 million justify.

ADAM DUNN AND HIS TRULY AWFUL SEASON

Until Adam Dunn came around, nobody fully understood that the power source of a baseball slugger just might reside inside his appendix. But in 2011, after Dunn had signed a remarkably generous $56 million contract over four seasons with the White Sox (representing about 10 percent of Chicago's payroll each season), his self-confidence and lethal swing were somehow extracted along with the supposedly unnecessary little tube. It happened quickly, inexplicably.

When Dunn arrived in Chicago, he started out fine. He knocked a homer on Opening Day and was 4 for 15 with five RBIs in his first four games, before the appendix flared up in early April and he underwent emergency surgery. Dunn was out for about a week, came back, and was suddenly pathetic. Like Samson shorn of his locks, Dunn was nothing without the appendix. The left-handed batter had trouble with righties and couldn't hit lefties at all, going 0 for 30 against them during one stretch. From 2010 to 2011, he dropped more than .100 points on his batting average, to .159. He struck out 177 times in 415 at-bats and managed only eleven homers all season. As he unraveled, Dunn became bewildered and impatient. "This is ridiculous," he said at mid-season. "My family is frustrated, everyone. I don't even answer my phone anymore because I don't want to hear what's wrong with this and that. I can't even put it into words. This is ridiculous."

Chicago's hitting coach, Greg Walker, tried changing Dunn's stance and his stride. His bat speed was fine, and he wasn't necessarily swinging at bad pitches. "I'm taking the balls and swinging at strikes," Dunn said. He was just missing, fouling off mistake pitches. He changed bat models and bat colors. Dunn listened to suggestions from the media. "I've pulled out all the stops for you," he told reporters. He was so historically awful that Dunn flirted constantly with the record books. His 177 strikeouts set a franchise record, topping Dave Nicholson's 175. His batting average for the year would have been recorded as the lowest for a regular position player on any club in the major leagues since Bill Bergen's .139 in 1909, except that sore knees and benchings against lefties kept Dunn's total plate appearances to 496, while a player required 502 to qualify officially for consideration. Because Dunn was acquired as a designated hitter, his numbers were especially abhorrent.

The White Sox surely hadn't signed Dunn for his glove. Considered one of the worst outfielders in baseball, Dunn held the record for errors among active left fielders. The Nationals moved him to first base, where he was nearly adequate, and Chicago's manager, Ozzie Guillén, slotted him at DH. Dunn was a burly fellow, six feet six and about 285 pounds, nicknamed Big Donkey. And right through 2010, he could hit. He slammed thirty-eight homers with 103 RBIs that season, receiving votes for MVP. Dunn trailed only Albert Pujols in total homers over seven seasons from 2004 to 2010.

There had been some red flags with Dunn, however, that the White Sox probably should have spotted. He always struck out too much. He had been scolded by pundits and officials over the years for what appeared to be a lack of passion for the game. Dunn also wasn't known to work on his hitting during the off-season, though he said that would change. "Just have to keep battling," he said. By 2012, Dunn had regained all facets of his game, good and bad. The homers and strikeouts were plentiful. The 2011 season was just a surreal memory. Whether the White Sox were getting their $54 million worth, however, remained debatable.

MIKE HAMPTON AND DENNY NEAGLE, THE $172 MILLION TANDEM

In December 2000, the Colorado Rockies went on one of the greatest, and dumbest, spending sprees in the history of professional sports. Looking to revamp their tattered rotation, they first inked Denny Neagle to a five-year, $51 million contract. Eight days later, on December 12, they signed Mike Hampton to an eight-year, $121 million deal, which was then the largest in sports history. They were suddenly committed to $172 million to two lefty starters unlikely to retain or regain peak form. Neagle was thirty-two years old, coming off a 7-7 season and a 5.81 ERA with the Yanks. Hampton was just twenty-eight, but he was more than a year removed from his near–Cy Young season with the Astros and was accustomed to playing in pitcher-friendly ballparks. These moves set back the Colorado franchise several years, at least until the Rockies reinvented themselves in part by trading away Hampton in 2002.

When he first signed his outrageous pact, Hampton insulted the intelligence of most everyone by claiming one of the main reasons he came to Denver was the school system for his two sons, including a one-year-old. His agent, Mark Rodgers, also said the decision was not about the money. "It's always about the money," said Steve Phillips, the former general manager of the Mets. "Especially when it's not about the money." During his two expensive seasons in Colorado, Hampton went 21-28 with an ERA of 5.75. The thin aerodynamics of Coors Field played with his head as he gave up fifty-five homers in two seasons. He had yielded a total of only twenty-two homers the previous two years at two pitchers' paradises, the Astrodome and Shea Stadium. His control, always a problem, grew shakier in Denver. The relocation to Coors did improve one facet of Hampton's game: he batted .315 with ten homers those two seasons. That, of course, was not why the Rockies had signed him, so they dealt Hampton in November 2002 with Juan Pierre to the Marlins for Preston Wilson, Vic Darensbourg, Charles Johnson, and Pablo Ozuna. Wilson produced 141 RBIs the very next season to lead the National League.

Looking back on the big contract when he retired in 2010, Hampton said it had weighed on him considerably. "It's unfortunate," he said. "I've thought about it quite a bit. Shoot, when I sign a big contract, I want to be underpaid, not overpaid. Even though I wasn't as successful as I would have liked, it wasn't from lack of trying or lack of work or lack of want. . . . I can look in the mirror and face the guy looking back and know he's telling the truth."

Neagle's story was different, sadder in many respects. He had been on top of the world in 1997, when he went 20-5 with a 2.97 ERA over 233⅓ innings, finishing third in the National League Cy Young voting. A former All-Star with the Pirates, he had four pitches and reliable control. Neagle was an amiable fellow, well liked by teammates. He would make sure to watch a movie the night before each start. Not the standard *Rocky* stuff, either. One of his favorite films was *The Sound of Music,* and Neagle would admit to it in a moment. "I'm comfortable enough with my masculinity," he told ESPN.com. But by 2000, Neagle was clearly not the same pitcher, traded around and struggling while with the Reds and the Yankees. The Rockies ignored all the warning signs. Plagued by injuries, Neagle, the former iron man, went just 19-23 with a 5.57 ERA in seventy-two games over the next three seasons in Colorado. He won the Rockies' Good Guy Award, and little else. Neagle needed reconstructive surgery on his left elbow in July 2003 and underwent surgery for a torn left labrum in June 2004, missing that season entirely. Then, in November 2004, in a terribly embarrassing and public incident, he was charged by police in a Denver suburb with soliciting a prostitute. A woman riding in his Cadillac Escalade—the vehicle of choice for major-league millionaires—said he paid her $40 for oral sex early one morning. Neagle had been pulled over for speeding at the time, and his pants belt was reportedly unbuckled. He said he was just trying to get comfortable, but the prostitute offered it was more than that. That $40 eventually cost Neagle nearly $20 million, because the Rockies leaped at the opportunity to cancel his contract by citing a morals clause.

"While we are saddened by the circumstances surrounding Denny Neagle, our organization has and will continue to place great emphasis on character and accountability," said Keli McGregor, the Rockies' team president. One can only wonder if the Rockies might not have been quite as concerned about Neagle's character if he had won twenty games in 2004. Neagle eventually pleaded guilty to one count of patronizing a prostitute and was sentenced to forty hours of community service. The event reportedly doomed his marriage. Finally, there was one last bit of disgrace, and an indication of Neagle's desperation in the latter years of his career. Neagle was mentioned in the 2007 *Mitchell Report*. Kirk Radomski said Neagle had contacted him in 2000, seeking human growth hormone. Radomski told investigators he sold Neagle HGH and steroids five or six times and produced eight checks from or on behalf of the pitcher.

By the time of *The Mitchell Report* in 2007, the Rockies had extricated themselves from the contracts of both Hampton and

Neagle. Their player payroll was the fifth lowest in the major leagues, and they'd also won the pennant that year.

OLIVER PÉREZ AND OVERSTAYING ONE'S WELCOME

It isn't often a cash-strapped team facing potential bankruptcy from a billion-dollar lawsuit will swallow $12 million just to get rid of a player. But that's what the Mets' ownership did at the start of the 2011 season, cutting Ollie Pérez at the insistence of howling fans and media members who had seen more than enough wayward pitches from the lefty starter. The saga of Pérez and his $36 million contract is a lesson for all general managers: don't fall in love with a pitcher's stuff if that stuff can't find the plate. Pérez owned a lively ninety-two-mile-per-hour four-seam fastball and a slider with plenty of movement. Unfortunately, he often had no idea where the ball was going. In 2008, just before the general manager, Omar Minaya, offered Pérez this exorbitant three-year pact, the pitcher had led the league with 105 walks in 194 innings while hitting eleven batters. Minaya continued to believe Pérez might be cured of this wildness. After all, the pitcher had been extremely effective, and clutch, during the Mets' 2007 regular season run to the National League Championship Series. But there was no science behind Minaya's faith. Young pitchers with control problems can often evolve and learn the fine art of location—Sandy Koufax being the prime example. Pitchers who grow wild in mid-career and without any obvious physical problem, though, rarely recover from the affliction. Pérez had already been in the league for seven seasons when his control deserted him. It certainly appeared to be largely a mental problem with Pérez, who would suddenly implode at any moment in a game after three or four solid innings. The Wilpons were not yet being sued for their investment gains by the victims of the Bernie Madoff scheme, so Minaya was given enough payroll to take the risk.

What followed was an utter public relations fiasco. To begin with, Pérez had mopey body language, exuding a sense of indifference that did not go over well with fans. After lousy appearances, he would merely shrug—not the demonstration of penitence demanded by the New York audience. On May 6, 2009, just two months after he'd signed the overblown pact, Pérez was placed on the disabled list with patellar tendinitis in his right knee and didn't return to action for another two months. He aggravated the same injury and in August underwent surgery that ended his season. For the year, Pérez was 3-4 with a 6.82 ERA in fourteen starts, walking fifty-eight batters in sixty-six innings. The next season was worse, if that is possible. His seventh start of the season on May 14 in Florida stood out as the quintessential disaster. Pérez gave up nine hits and seven earned runs while walking three in just three and one-third innings. Ill-fated manager Jerry Manuel immediately moved Pérez to the bullpen, where he fared no better.

Desperate to salvage something from a contract that was becoming more embarrassing by the moment, Minaya asked Pérez to accept a minor-league assignment so that coaches there could work with him on his problems. Pérez declined the invitation, a veto that was his contractual right as a veteran with more than five years of major-league service. This was now becoming a horror show for the Mets' management, which asked him again to do the right thing. Pérez refused again and was suspiciously placed on the disabled list with an alleged irritation of an old tendinitis problem. In this way, the Mets could call up a replacement on their active roster while pushing Pérez out of sight for fifteen days. Major-league officials understandably wondered whether this medical development was real or manufactured. After an inquiry, the league allowed the transaction to stand. Eventually, hoping to gain some pop on his fastball, Pérez agreed to a stint in Port St. Lucie to pitch some minor-league innings. He returned to the Mets on August 30 but pitched a total of only three and one-third more innings in relief the rest of the season. "A lot of times [the New York effect] can be overstated," Minaya said. "Each place has its own uniqueness. Some players like the Northeast because of the intensity of the fan base. Some can't play in the cold. You do ask the questions to different scouts: Do you think the guy can pitch in New York? Most guys can handle this. Some guys try too hard. When things spin out of control, they can't get back on track."

Pérez's failures were so epic they greatly contributed to the reassignment of Minaya and the hiring of the general manager Sandy Alderson. This, in turn, finally allowed the Mets to turn the page on Pérez. Alderson released him in March 2011 after an unimpressive spring training and before the start of the regular season. His velocity was down, on top of everything else.

"They told me they were going to let me go, and I think that is best for the team and best for me," Pérez said. "The people everywhere are free to say all that stuff. I know I did everything I can to get better, and the result doesn't work right. The fans pay to see us play. I think I can do better than that, and that's why I'm not going to quit. I want to get better, for my family and me."

Eventually, Perez resurfaced as a reliever in Seattle. New York fans didn't care much about Pérez's outings, as long as they were nowhere near Citi Field.

CHAN HO WRONG-PARK

Chan Ho Park is a textbook example of someone who appeared imposing on the mound of a pitcher's park and then decomposed when moved to a hitter's bandbox. Unfortunately for the Texas Rangers, they bought big-time into Park's alluring performances at Dodger Stadium, where he was coming off 18-10 and 15-11 seasons with ERAs of 3.27 and 3.50. Park, a power pitcher with dubious control, threw to contact and used the oversized outfield to his advantage in Los Angeles. He was twenty-eight years old and viewed as a dependable workhorse, having thrown more than two hundred innings in three of the previous four years. Park was also considered a bad-ass battler: in 1999 he karate-kicked the pitcher Tim Belcher after a rough tag and was suspended for seven games.

John Hart, general manager of the Rangers, jumped through hoops in 2002 to sign Park to the sixth-largest contract ever at the time for a pitcher, $65 million over five years. The Rangers were desperate. In 2001, they had the third-best hitting team in the league while ranking dead last in pitching with a horrific staff ERA of 5.71. Only one of six starters that season had an ERA under 5.00, and four were above 6.00. Alex Rodríguez, rarely known as the most self-sacrificing of men, agreed to slightly restructure his ten-year, $252 million contract with Texas in order to bring Park aboard. "They came to me and asked if I had any flexibility, and I said I'm a gymnast if that's what it takes to get pitchers," Rodríguez said at Park's introductory press conference. At the same session, Rafael Palmeiro declared, "He's the ace we've been looking for."

Park tried hard to fit in. "I'm going to put on my hat and boots, then we're going to bring a ring to the Texas Rangers," he said. But after his first six games with Texas that season, his ERA was 10.94, and he never even remotely found his groove. His pitches were all over the place, and suddenly it dawned on people that Park might not have the best pitch location in the world. He managed to lead the league in hit batsmen (seventeen) in 2002, while pitching just 145⅔ innings. There was nothing that could be done for him despite an assortment of adjustments. To complicate matters, Park suffered a series of injuries, throwing just 29⅔ innings in 2003 with an ERA of 7.58. Altogether, Park's four-season numbers in Texas—before he was dumped on San Diego—were a big reason the Rangers never finished better than third place during those years. He was 22-23 there, with a 5.79 ERA in 68 games and 380⅔ innings pitched. Even after trading Park, Texas couldn't escape the hex. The Rangers received in return Phil Nevin, who batted .182 with eight RBIs for them on his own steep contract.

Park, it turned out, had one more surge remaining in his right arm. It came, not surprisingly, when he returned for the 2008 season to Dodger Stadium. There, he posted a 3.40 ERA in fifty-four appearances as a reliever and spot starter. On June 27, three days short of his thirty-fifth birthday, he positively sparkled during a seven-strikeout, four-hit, no-run start over six innings. Park's impressive record as a Dodger over his career was 84-58. "A little bit of everything," Park said, explaining his success in Los Angeles. "A little bit mechanics, a better mentality. Better family support. Better city? Better teammates? I don't know. I had some injuries. When you're healthy, it's easier to trust yourself."

It's also easier when the power alleys are deep, foul territory is expansive, and the night air is heavy.

JASON SCHMIDT AND COVETING THY NEIGHBOR'S PITCHER

Few ballplayers cheat time, least of all major-league pitchers. There have been some exceptions over the years who retained their fastball or were able to adjust to waning physical talents through deception. Most of them, however, are not Nolan Ryan or Greg Maddux. They become a crapshoot once they enter their mid-thirties, which is why the Los Angeles Dodgers should have known better when they signed Jason Schmidt to a three-year, $47 million contract for the 2007 season at the age of thirty-four.

Schmidt had given the Dodgers considerable false hope. He threw over two hundred innings in three of the previous four seasons for their rivals, the San Francisco Giants. During an All-Star 2003 season, he went 17-5 with a 2.34 ERA and was second in the National League Cy Young voting. He started two games of the 2002 World Series, then threw a shutout in Game 1 of the 2003 National League Division Series.

Schmidt paid off for the Giants, and then some, on a five-year, $41 million deal. Maybe just as important, he had been murder on the Dodgers. Even in 2006, not his best season, Schmidt made six-out-of-six quality starts against Los Angeles, allowing no more than three runs and lasting at least six innings in each of those appearances. He also struck out sixteen batters against the Marlins that June, inspiring a plaque that still sits behind right field at AT&T Park. When he became a free agent after that season, the Dodgers leaped at the opportunity to strip their hated rivals of this pitcher. It would, in theory, be a double blow to San Francisco: the Giants would lose a top starter; the Dodgers would gain one. Schmidt signed for $47 million, and the general manager, Ned Colletti, felt very good about his baseball team. "Jason is a top-of-the-rotation starter who can dominate a game as well as any pitcher in the major leagues," Colletti said after the ink dried. "He's a proven winner, and that's something very hard to find."

Actually, it would be hard to find a free agent who ever fell apart quicker than Schmidt. He had one decent outing in April against the Brewers. He was then abused by the Rockies and the Padres before getting placed on the disabled list for forty-five days with right shoulder problems. He came back in June, with identical results. One good start, followed by two disasters and a return to the DL. Exploratory surgery led to the discovery that damage to his shoulder was worse than had been thought, and he required the rest of 2007 and all of 2008 to recover, assigned to a few minor-league rehab starts and nothing more. He still harbored hope at this juncture of reinventing himself as a control pitcher. "I'm not going to be the ninety-six, ninety-eight [mile

per hour] guy I was before," he said. "I just have to get it around
the plate and get them to hit it on the ground." Instead, they
hit his pitches for line drives, or over walls. After a disheartening spring training, Schmidt was again placed on the DL for the
start of 2009. When he finally returned on July 20, 2009, for his
first major-league game in more than two years, the pattern was
familiar. He pitched respectably against Cincinnati, then was
terrible in his next outing. There was one final burst of hope, a
six-inning shutout stint against the Braves. But in early August,
Schmidt was once again on the DL, and Joe Torre, the Dodgers' manager, began speaking of Schmidt's baseball career in the
past tense. "I just think the fact that he was able to come back
after two years and take the ball four times, that was something
that he was satisfied with," Torre said.

Altogether with the Dodgers, Schmidt started ten games
and went 3-6 with an ERA of 6.02 in forty-three and one-third
innings. Los Angeles had paid about $15.7 million for each of his
three wins and $1.1 million for each of his pitched innings.

DARREN DREIFORT, THE HOMEGROWN MISCALCULATION

General managers don't always make their mistakes while chasing other teams' free agents. Sometimes, they don't recognize
the medical ambush that awaits them right under their noses.
Consider the case of the injury-riddled Darren Dreifort, the
Dodgers pitcher who was coming off a decent, if unspectacular, season in 2000 at 12-9 with a 4.16 ERA and 164 strikeouts
in 192⅔ innings. For some reason, the general manager, Kevin
Malone, eagerly offered a five-year, $55 million deal to the agent
Scott Boras, who was threatening to make a deal for Dreifort
with the Rockies. The only holdup at the time, really, was that
Boras was negotiating a much bigger pact at those winter meetings on behalf of Alex Rodríguez. Dreifort was in his prime at

age twenty-eight, and the pitchers' market was slim at the time, yet his career numbers—39-45 and a 4.28 ERA—hardly seemed to justify such enthusiasm on the part of Malone. Dreifort had a history of medical troubles and had already missed an entire season in 1995. But the Dodgers had picked Dreifort second overall in the 1993 draft and invested seven years in his development. He had spent his entire professional career in Los Angeles, never pitching a day in the minors or learning his craft without major-league pressure.

Suffice it to say that things did not go well. Dreifort was ineffective when he was slotted into the Dodgers' No. 3 spot in the rotation. His very first start in 2001, on Tommy Lasorda Bobblehead Doll Day, foretold of a very shaky future. In the fifth inning against Arizona, with two outs and a runner on second, Dreifort gave up four successive hits, a walk, then another hit. Altogether, he allowed ten hits and six earned runs in four and two-thirds innings during that game against Arizona. He was 4-7 with a 5.13 ERA in 2001 before he was shut down in July, requiring reconstructive elbow surgery that kept him out the next season as well. During the entire span of Dreifort's new contract, the pitcher would start only twenty-six games, pitch just 205⅔ innings, with a record of 9-15 and an ERA of 4.64. Dreifort suffered major injuries along the way, requiring a series of surgeries and missing all of 2002 and 2005.

The Dodgers' staff of doctors and trainers had apparently missed some structural problems that would soon sabotage Dreifort's career. The poor fellow was clearly a medical morass. He reportedly suffered from a degenerative condition that weakened the connective tissues in his body. In addition to elbow and shoulder problems, he had knee and hip troubles. Before retiring prematurely at age thirty-two, Dreifort endured a dozen surgeries on his knee, hip, shoulder, and ankle. Dr. Marc Philippon, a surgeon from Vail, Colorado, who performed two operations on Dreifort's hip, said Dreifort had a deformity in his femur, or thighbone, that had led to his hip problems and prevented the pitcher from rotating properly during delivery. This in turn might have created problems with the elbow and knee.

When Dreifort showed up one day in retirement as a guest minor-league instructor in Arizona, he told MLB.com he was enjoying his role as full-time father to three kids. "Some days I feel like I could still play," he said. "Some days I feel like I got run over by a truck. My hip and knee still give me trouble. I figured maybe [my career] was supposed to end. I got divorced and needed to be home to be with my kids. I haven't regretted that at all."

The Dodgers, on the other hand, had fifty-five million regrets.

MO VAUGHN, TOO FAT TO BAT

Most teams commit their biggest errors involving free agency when judging pitchers, the toughest breed to figure. The New York Mets, though, have made a curious habit in recent years of acquiring and overpaying position players. That would include the likes of Bobby Bonilla, Roberto Alomar, Jason Bay, and the ultimate sucker buy, Mo Vaughn. Vaughn was halfway through a six-year, $80 million contract he'd signed in December 1998 with the Angels when the Mets foolishly acquired him at age thirty-four before the 2002 season in a trade for their own consistent starter Kevin Appier. Vaughn's deal was back-loaded, too. The Mets, in theory, might have owed the big first baseman more than $46 million over his final three seasons.

The deal was enthusiastically endorsed by the general manager, Steve Phillips, even though Vaughn had missed the entire previous season with knees that were already arthritic. Phillips and the Mets' manager, Bobby Valentine, went to watch Vaughn hit off a tee in a Connecticut batting cage and apparently were impressed by his sheer power. But when Vaughn showed up for spring training at 268 pounds, the bloom was quickly off the rose. Already a lousy fielder, he had grown substantially creakier. It seemed crazy that he wasn't playing in the American League, where he could still be an effective designated hitter.

The onetime MVP managed to appear in 139 games for the Mets in 2002, batting .259 with twenty-six homers—including one late-season shot that banged impressively against the Budweiser scoreboard at Shea. But he struck out 145 times in 487 at-bats and was costing his team many runs defensively at first base. The next year, Vaughn was able to play only twenty-seven games before going on the disabled list in early May with joint and cartilage damage to his knee. He had become something of a caricature in New York, contributing in no small part to Phillips's firing that June.

Vaughn retired officially in January 2004. "I'm through, man," he said at a Boston baseball banquet, reported the *Globe*. "My career is over. I have an injury no doctor can fix. It doesn't look good at all. It's a bad situation. I worked hard this off-season trying to

It was asking an awful lot for portly Mo Vaughn to bend down for a ground ball at first base.
AP Photo/M. Spencer Green

put strength in the knee. An athlete knows his body. You know pain. You feel it in your bones. You've got to get up, get on with life, and keep moving." At least the Mets were able to recover 75 percent of his 2004 salary from insurance, no small consolation for an ownership group about to face financial problems. Vaughn went on to become a major investor in New York City housing redevelopment. Unfortunately, he was also named in *The Mitchell Report* for allegedly purchasing performance-enhancing drugs from Kirk Radomski back in 2001, when he was hoping to return from his injuries while with the Angels. Those drugs reportedly were human growth hormone, not diet pills.

RUSS ORTIZ AND THE BIG BUYOUT

When it comes to instant breakdowns, it is tough to top the odd case of Russ Ortiz. The righty starter had gone 36-16 over his previous two years in Atlanta, finishing fourth in the Cy Young voting in 2003. He became a free agent at the close of the 2004 season at age thirty and was considered one of the big prizes available during the off-season. The Diamondbacks were a terrible team at the time, coming off a dreadful 111-loss season, searching for someone to replace the ace Randy Johnson, who had just signed with the Yanks. Ortiz was a local Phoenix resident. The general manager, Joe Garagiola Jr., believed Ortiz could become a big part of the franchise's wholesale reinvention. Arizona was on a spending spree, with the full backing of its owners. Just a day before, the D-Backs had signed another big-name free agent, Troy Glaus, to a four-year, $45 million contract.

"We have told you over the last couple of months repeatedly that our intent is not to rebuild, but to reload," said Ken Kendrick, the team's lead investor at the time. "We are reloading. We told you our intent was to be competitive and we're going to be."

Unfortunately, Ortiz quickly transformed into a terrible embarrassment. An injured rib sabotaged his first season in Arizona, as he went 5-11 with a 6.89 ERA in just twenty-two appearances. He only got worse in 2006. After six starts he was 0-5 with a 7.54 ERA, which made him 1-14 over his previous nineteen starts. The Diamondbacks then made an astounding cut-their-losses decision, releasing Ortiz while they were still on the hook for $22 million. This represented the largest sum ever swallowed by a team upon a player's release. "I broke a record. I have that going for me," Ortiz would joke years later, after retiring.

For the D-Backs, it was no joke. Circumstances had met the two criteria for such drastic action. Ortiz had been terrible. Just as important, Arizona had a new general manager who was not responsible for the original contract. No GM would ever cut bait and admit to such a grievous error if that error were his. "We're like most clubs: Every dollar counts. You want to spend them as effectively as possible," said the new GM, Josh Byrnes, about Ortiz's release. "That affected the decision, but we also were true to ourselves, and we want to put our best twenty-five on the field and try to win games. Obviously, we owe Russ a lot of money going forward."

Ortiz tried in vain to reinvent his career, signing on with another bad team, Baltimore, for the remainder of the season. The Orioles had little to lose, they figured, getting a $22 million pitcher for virtually nothing. He was even worse, if that is possible, going 0-3 with an 8.48 ERA. For that memorable 2006 season, his totals were 0-8 in twenty-six appearances with an 8.14 ERA. He would hook on with the Giants, Astros, and Dodgers, faring little better after Tommy John surgery. Give him some credit: at this juncture, Ortiz was playing for the sheer love of the game, earning a paltry $380,000 from the Giants in 2007. Maybe because every GM always thinks he can unearth buried talent, Ortiz found five different homes during his final five seasons in the majors, never posting an ERA under 5.51 for any of those years.

As a postscript, the Glaus signing was no great shakes for Arizona, either. Glaus was a great success at the plate, hitting thirty-seven homers with ninety-seven RBIs in 2005. But he was a horrendous third baseman, committing twenty-four errors with a major-league-worst .946 fielding percentage. And while the Diamondbacks needed Glaus's power, the failure of Ortiz meant they required a starting pitcher even more. Glaus was dealt to

Toronto with Sergio Santos for Miguel Batista and Orlando Hudson, a pleasant surprise at second base. Batista, however, was a washout during his second, one-season tenure with Arizona and left in 2006 as a free agent. Meanwhile, Glaus went on to hit thirty-eight homers with 104 RBIs in 2006 with the Blue Jays. In this way, Ortiz was the gift that just kept re-gifting, to everyone but the Diamondbacks.

BOTTOM TEN

1   **BARRY ZITO**   A seven-year, $133 million flop.

2   **ADAM DUNN**   Lost an appendix, then the power swing. The power came back. The appendix didn't.

3   **MIKE HAMPTON**   Who signs a pitcher for eight years?

4   **DENNY NEAGLE**   At least he was cheaper than Hampton.

5   **OLIVER PÉREZ**   Ollie didn't cause all the Mets' woes—it just seemed that way.

6   **CHAN HO PARK**   Change of venue meant change of fortune.

7   **JASON SCHMIDT**   Golden arm grew tinny for Dodgers.

8   **DARREN DREIFORT**   Injury problems, before and after he signed for $55 million.

9   **MO VAUGHN**   Not worth the weight, or the money.

10   **(tie) RUSS ORTIZ JASON BAY**   (Ortiz) So bad, he was released despite the contract. (Bay) Signed four-year, $66 million pact with the Mets, and then started running into walls.

6 | WHAT'S AN EMERY BOARD?
The Biggest Cheaters of All Time

PERFORMANCE-ENHANCING DRUGS AREN'T the only way to cheat, and they certainly aren't the most imaginative method. The best cheaters in baseball, historically speaking, are some of the best innovators in the game. They taught everyone how to cork bats, carve up baseballs, steal signs, and tug on uniforms. They mastered the aerodynamics of a slimy sinker. They refined the fine arts of the phantom double-play relay and the phantom tag at home plate. And one of them even crawled through stadium heating vents on his notable mission of mischief.

GAYLORD PERRY AND HIS VASELINE

Gaylord Perry, a Hall of Famer, really doesn't belong in a book of worsts. But he was just so naughty it's hard to ignore him. Perry titled his autobiography *Me and the Spitter,* which is a good indication the pitcher was involved in something wet and unsavory during his twenty-two-year major-league career. The great miracle is only that Perry somehow logged twenty-one of those seasons before he was ejected for his bad habit on August 23, 1982, and disciplined for doctoring a baseball.

Some historical background on the spitball is necessary here. It should be noted that the pitch does not necessarily involve actual saliva and that it was not always illegal. The spitball was first invented in the late nineteenth century by several pitchers and truly popularized by Big Ed Walsh, an extremely effective American League pitcher in the early twentieth century for the Chicago White Sox. Back then, real spit—often mixed with tobacco chaw or infield dirt—was the doctoring agent of choice. Since umpires did not replace baseballs with the neurotic, compulsive frequency of umpires today, pitchers often used this method simply to darken the balls and therefore make them harder for batters to spot. When managers at a winter meeting voted to ban spitballs for the 1920 season, they did so with great consideration for existing practitioners. Teams were permitted to designate two pitchers as spitballers who could continue to muck up baseballs. After that 1920 season, the pitch was banished entirely, although seventeen spitballers were granted exemptions through a grandfather clause. Over the years, as umpires examined baseballs more closely and games became televised, pitchers grew more secretive and resourceful. Spit was often replaced by other substances such as Vaseline or hair gel. The goo would alter the aerodynamics of a ball in flight, interfering with the conventional paths dictated by spin, speed, and the friction of seams. Pitches suddenly veered unexpectedly, most often downward from the hand of an expert.

Perry was in his third season with the Giants in 1964, he said, when he was first taught the merits of the spitball by his teammate Bob Shaw. Perry's numbers immediately began to improve dramatically. His ERA dipped from 4.03 in 1963 to 2.75 in 1964. As he honed his craft with Vaseline, Perry became universally known as the most famous spitballer in baseball. He was always coy about this, hoping his reputation would burrow into the heads of opposing batters, who didn't know exactly where the forkball ended and the Vaseline began. This drove especially Reggie Jackson insane. Jackson struck out twenty-two times against Perry during their careers. After fanning once against Perry when the pitcher was playing for the Mariners, Jackson went to the dugout, retrieved a container of water or Gatorade—

An umpire checks Gaylord Perry's cap for Vaseline or its generic equivalent. *AP Photo*

depending on the retelling—then splashed it on the field while complaining that Perry might as well use that liquid on the baseball as well.

"Reggie and I had some great competitions together," Perry said. "He'd hit some home runs off me and I'd tip my cap, but I got him thrown out of four games. He could hit anybody's fastball, but I'd throw him great forkballs. He'd think they were spitters and strike out. Reggie got very upset when he struck out. I think he didn't want to come up and hit against me again, so he'd get himself thrown out."

The balls that Perry threw were not only tough on batters. They were difficult for his catchers as well. Gene Tenace, who caught Perry in the late 1970s with the Padres, said he sometimes couldn't throw the baseballs back to the mound, let alone to second base, because they were so greasy. Finally, on August 23, 1982, Perry was nailed for his shenanigans and ejected from a game against the Red Sox. He was suspended for ten days, which did nothing to dim his spirits or his remarkable career stats. Perry finished with a record of 314-265, an ERA of 3.11, two Cy Youngs, and five All-Star Game selections. "He should be in the Hall of Fame with a tube of K-Y Jelly attached to his plaque," the manager Gene Mauch said. It took a while, but eventually Perry was elected to the Hall of Fame in 1991, as 342 out of 443 voters that year decided to forgive the spitter and honor his forkball.

JOE NIEKRO AND HIS DEEP POCKET

The late Joe Niekro was an affable and generous man who made the most of his middling talents and substantial time in the majors. He was a disarming cheater as well. Incontrovertible evidence of his mischief can be viewed on a popular video chronicling a Monday night incident in August 1987, after Niekro had thrown some suspiciously active knucklers for the Twins against the Angels.

The umpire Steve Palermo examines the baseball, notices some odd scratch marks, and orders Niekro to empty his pants pockets. Out comes a photograph of Niekro's son, for starters. What a dad! Palermo isn't satisfied. The pockets are further emptied, turned inside out, and suddenly Niekro discreetly flings an emery board several feet away from the inspection site. For an instant, it seems his teammate Kent Hrbek might rescue Niekro if he just picks up the nail file quickly and discards it. But Hrbek appears as puzzled as everyone else, and soon the second base umpire is tossing Niekro out of the game, while Joe has a bemused, guilty look on his face. There is also a small piece of sandpaper on the ground, shaped to fit a finger.

"The guy was so blatant," Palermo said. "It was like a guy walking down the street carrying a bottle of booze during Prohibition."

Niekro later insisted he was using the emery board to file his nails in the dugout. As for the sandpaper, he said, "Sometimes I sweat a lot, and the emery board gets wet. And I'll also use the paper for small blisters. I don't have to scuff a knuckleball. And I throw mainly knuckleballs. . . . If I've been illegal, I've been illegal for fifteen years."

Palermo cited the scuffed balls, however, as evidence there was malicious intent.

"They can carry a chain saw as long as they don't use it on the ball," he said.

Another umpire and forensics expert from that crew, Dave Phillips, reported the sandpaper was "contoured to fit a finger. I'm sure he had it stuck to a finger on his glove hand. When we examined the sandpaper, there was a fingerprint on the back side. The cuts on the baseball were sharp and with depth."

The umpires sent five scuffed baseballs to the league office, and the American League president, Dr. Bobby Brown, sided with the umps. The penalty was stiff, a ten-game suspension. Brown would not budge on appeal. "After considering all of the items presented by Joe Niekro and the Minnesota Twins, the suspension has been upheld and will commence today," Brown announced.

Say this much for Niekro: he had a well-developed sense

of humor. Upon returning to the team hotel after the game, he signed two nail files for a fan who was waiting in the lobby after driving nearly a hundred miles for the honor.

"Maybe I should go into the emery board business," Niekro said. "Half the people probably didn't know what an emery board was before this. . . . One of the guys on the team came up Monday night and said, 'What's an emery board?'"

During his suspension, Niekro appeared on *Late Night with David Letterman* while carrying a power sander, a fifty-foot extension cord, and an apron jammed with various filing materials. Some of these were gag gifts from his brother, Phil, whose knuckleballs also had their way of darting in highly unusual fashion. On the show, Joe revealed a piece of sandpaper with a message allegedly from his brother: "We've been using this in Cleveland. It works great. It has a peel-off back. Stick it inside your pocket and the umps will never find it."

There was a happy ending to all this for Niekro. He returned in late August, became eligible for the playoff roster, and capped off that season with two innings of one-hit relief work for Minnesota in the Twins' World Series victory over St. Louis. This represented the longest span of time in major-league history, from 1967 to 1987, between a player's first game and his first appearance in a World Series. Joe had already clinched the last laugh over his brother, in any case. In 973 career at-bats, Joe hit only one homer, and that came against Phil in 1976. No sandpaper was required for the feat, unless Phil was using it.

JASON GRIMSLEY, EXPLORER

Jason Grimsley was a flawed pitcher who somehow managed to endure for fifteen seasons on seven teams in the major leagues, despite a career record of 42-58 and a 4.77 ERA. But that is only a small part of the story with Grimsley, who was famously caught cheating in two very different ways—once in an appealing, folksy stunt and then again in more conventional, modern-day fashion.

Grimsley's first adventure occurred during a Cleveland-Chicago game on July 15, 1994, when he was a reliever for the Indians. Acting on a tip, the White Sox manager, Gene Lamont, went to the umpire Dave Phillips in the very first inning and challenged Albert Belle's bat, which Lamont correctly believed to be corked. The bat was taken by Phillips to the locked umpires' room for later inspection. The Indians knew the bat was illegal and hatched a plan to rescue Belle from an inevitable suspension. Grimsley, a tall, slim man with a penchant for pranks, would slither through an air duct that originated in the ceiling of the Indians' clubhouse and break into the umpires' dressing room. Once there, he would replace Belle's bat with an uncorked one belonging to his teammate Paul Sorrento. This would not be a perfect crime, because the new bat bore Sorrento's name, not Belle's. There was no getting around that problem, however, because every one of Belle's available bats was corked.

Corked, or juiced, bats were not in themselves a new development. Neither was insistent denial of that particular ploy. In 1974, Graig Nettles, the Yankees' third baseman, was caught using a bat infused with six Super Balls. When the bat exploded and spat out its illegal contents, Nettles insisted he was given the bat by a Chicago fan and had no idea what was inside. Grimsley, hoping to make Belle's bat disappear, shimmied his way through the duct with the aid of a flashlight he carried in his mouth while toting the substitute club. He was guided from below by a loyal Cleveland clubhouse attendant. "My heart was going 1,000 miles a second," Grimsley told *The New York Times* when he finally confessed to his action nearly five years later. "I went skydiving once, and I can compare it to that. I just rolled the dice, a crapshoot." Grimsley made it into the umpires' room, dropped down on a refrigerator, and replaced the bat. His mission was only temporarily successful. The umpires noticed the felony immediately, and Belle eventually gave himself up, along with the bats. A ten-game suspension was eventually reduced to seven games. Grimsley was never punished for the deed, despite his eventual admission.

Strange stuff was always happening around the impish Grimsley, not all of it so lighthearted. In January 2005, a small plane, a twin-engine Cessna, dropped from the sky one morning and crashed into the back patio of his Overland Park, Kansas, home. Grimsley's family was unharmed, though the pilot and four passengers all were killed in the horrendous crash.

And while the Belle bat escapade can be viewed as a welcome part of baseball lore, Grimsley's penchant for stretching the rules eventually caught up with him in far less charming fashion. In 2006, at the tail end of his career, Grimsley became the fourteenth major leaguer to be suspended for the use of performance-enhancing drugs. His home was raided by federal investigators searching for proof that he had distributed PEDs, including human growth hormone. ESPN divulged court documents showing Grimsley had failed a drug test in 2003. He was released by the Diamondbacks after admitting to the use of human growth hormone, steroids, and amphetamines. Some $875,000 of his salary was withheld. On June 12, 2006, Grimsley was suspended for fifty games for violation of baseball's Drug Prevention and Treatment Program. He would never pitch again.

Grimsley made his mark, even if his major-league career was far from impressive. He began as a starter for the Phillies in 1989, posting a 5.89 ERA. In his last season relieving for Arizona, he had a 4.88 ERA. He managed to pitch two and one-third innings for the Yankees during their 1999 World Series win over Atlanta, again finding himself where the action was. His greatest talent, though, was clearly as a bat burglar, crawling through the ducts.

WILTON GUERRERO, PICKING UP THE PIECES

Wilton Guerrero looked nothing like his robust younger brother Vladimir, whether he was swinging at the plate or merely modeling a uniform. Wilton was at least eighty pounds lighter during his playing days, a speedy utility infielder and part-time leadoff hitter, a journeyman for four teams over eight years with terrible power numbers. He struck out too much and would finish his career with eleven homers in 1,678 at-bats. This made the incident on June 1, 1997, all the more remarkable. When Guerrero was leading off for the Dodgers against the Cardinals in St. Louis, his bat splintered into several pieces. Instead of completing his run to first base on the groundout, the rookie headed directly for the head of the bat lying in the infield. This detour was so suspicious that the home plate umpire, Steve Rippley, decided to investigate the precious chunk of wood. Upon mutual inspection, Rippley and the third-

Plate umpire Steve Rippley scoops up the remnants of Wilton Guerrero's corked bat before the hitter can do so himself, leading to an eight-game suspension for the Dodgers' second baseman. *AP Photo/Leon Algee*

base ump, Bruce Froemming, quickly concluded the bat was corked—despite the futile protestation by the Dodgers' third-base coach, Mike Scioscia, that the substance was probably just mold. "The cork was right in there. There was no way to hide it," Froemming said.

At this time, Guerrero had only one homer in his major-league career. Rippley couldn't suppress a smile on the field, and even the Dodgers found themselves giggling a bit at the surreal situation. "It was the weirdest thing I've ever seen," said Mike Piazza, the Dodgers' catcher. "He's the last guy I thought I'd see use a corked bat. I had to go out there and see it myself."

Caught red-handed, Guerrero immediately confessed, though he insisted through a translator, his coach Manny Mota, this was the only instance when he'd ever done such a silly thing. "Anytime you do something wrong, the good Lord embarrasses you," Guerrero said. "It was the first time I used that kind of bat." Eventually, he was suspended for eight games and fined $1,000. The rookie found it difficult to sit out those days, sleeping off the guilt. "When you take eight days off and don't play, you get tired more easily," he said. After Guerrero returned, he completed what would be his finest season. He batted .291 with nine triples, a .403 slugging average, thirty-two RBIs, and a .989 fielding percentage at second base. These were modest zeniths, but Guerrero came close to matching those numbers only in 1998 and 2000. After a humbling season with two minor-league teams, he retired in 2005 and became a scout for the Dodgers in the Dominican Republic. Guerrero will forever be remembered as Vlad's thinner, older brother and the rookie whose infield housekeeping created a terrible mess.

KEVIN GROSS MISCONDUCT

Kevin Gross posted more wins than losses in only four of his fifteen major-league seasons. The starter was an admirable workhorse and once threw a no-hitter for the Dodgers against the Giants, but he led the league in some very bad categories along the way: home runs allowed (in 1986), walks issued (in 1988), hit batsmen (in 1986, 1987, and 1988), earned runs allowed (in 1989), and losses (in 1995). In his final three seasons with Texas and Anaheim, Gross's ERA ballooned to 5.54, 5.22, and 6.75. What he will always be remembered for, however, is his chutzpah.

On August 10, 1987, Gross was pitching against the Cubs at Veterans Stadium in Philadelphia when he was ejected in the top of the fifth inning for concealing sandpaper in his glove and scuffing baseballs. His pitches were sinking sharply, suspiciously. With two men on base, Chicago's manager, Gene Michael, appealed to the home plate ump, Charlie Williams, and the crew chief, John Kibler, demanding an inspection of Gross's mitt. Michael had been waiting for this moment, after collecting a dozen scuffed baseballs from Gross's previous outing against the Cubs at Wrigley Field. It was immediately clear to the umps in Philly that Gross was audaciously cheating—pulling a Joe Niekro, who had been nailed less than two weeks earlier for the same violation. "We went and looked at the glove, and there was a piece of emery paper or sandpaper glued in the glove," Kibler said. "It was right in the heel of the glove. It wasn't taped. I would say it was glued. I have seen it in the glove before. I have the glove, and I will take it to [National League president] Mr. Bart Giamatti."

After the game, Gross issued a nondenial denial, arguing only that he shouldn't have been examined in the first place. Gross was like a drunk driver insisting he wasn't speeding. Why was he being stopped?

"There's no reason to check me because the ball wasn't doing anything," Gross said. "I guess Gene Michael thought there was. I don't need anything in my glove. I was just out there having fun. I just don't think they had any reason to check me. That's all I have to say now. I'll have something to say later."

What followed was an intriguing battle of semantics. Giamatti suspended Gross for ten days, as expected. The Players Association appealed that penalty, on the grounds that the umpires found no scuffed balls and therefore no cheating had actually taken place. Gross initially resisted the appeal, then endorsed it. The Phillies were happy to go along with such a process. By delaying the suspension, they could soon replace Gross when rosters were expanded on September 1. Sure enough, things worked out perfectly for the club, not so much for Gross. Giamatti denied the appeal on September 1. The Phillies withheld Gross's $23,000 salary for that period, which was their option, and donated it to research for ALS, Lou Gehrig's disease, a charity organized in part by the Phillies' wives. Instead of shutting up about it and minimizing the public relations damage—or having fun with the scandal, like Niekro—Gross carped on about the decision. "I don't agree with it and I can't believe that my own club is penalizing me for something that I didn't do by taking my pay," Gross said. "Sandpaper in my glove has never done anything to help my career or make it any worse. It's something I just happened to play around with just recently, but never in a ballgame. And I'm a victim of it. They just got the wrong guy. I was in the wrong spot in the wrong time. There's a lot more to this than just me being suspended for the sandpaper incident."

Gross was vulnerable to criticism just on his performance alone (9-16, 4.35 ERA in 1987). Mike Schmidt, the team's star third baseman, emphatically turned on Gross. "It was just a matter of our guy being caught sort of red-handed," Schmidt said. "And under those circumstances, I would say a suspension was due and probably warranted. It's going to hurt him in the pocketbook, and if there are any other pitchers that have that habit, they'll probably think twice about it."

Gross never quite got over the incident. For years, he pestered the commissioner's office, demanding his glove be returned to its rightful owner. In August 1991, finally, the National League office returned his mitt. "Every year I've questioned about where it was, but I got the runaround and never heard too much about it," said Gross, by then a reliever for the Dodgers. "I think they had to go to Giamatti's house to get it, and that his wife had to find it."

BOTTOM TEN

1   **GAYLORD PERRY**   He was to the spitball what Mozart was to the opera.

2   **JOE NIEKRO**   Shameless, hilarious cheat.

3   **JASON GRIMSLEY**   Found a new way of venting.

4   **JOHN McGRAW**   Before he became a manager, the infielder would grab opposing runners by the belt to slow them down on the base paths.

5   **DON SUTTON**   Dodger pitcher taunted umps in search of sandpaper by putting a note in his glove: "You're getting close, but it's not here."

6   **WILTON GUERRERO**   Should have run to first instead of collecting his juiced bat.

7   **KEVIN GROSS**   Gets major points for demanding his tainted glove back from the commissioner.

8   **NORM CASH**   Long after he won the American League batting title in 1961, the former Tiger star admitted he customized his bat with glue and cork.

9   **ALBERT BELLE**   His bats were corked, and half the league knew it.

10   **(tie) PREACHER ROE JOEL PERALTA**   (Roe) The former Brooklyn Dodger ace admitted to *Sports Illustrated*, "The outlawed spitball was my money pitch." (Peralta) After getting ejected in 2012 for pine tar in his mitt, the Rays' pitcher taunted the Nationals, "Good for them. They still lose the game."

7 | NUMBER ⅛
The Oddest Ballplayers of All Time

THERE HAVE BEEN major-league players who didn't so much play their way onto rosters as wake up one day to discover they were at the wrong address, reporting for a job they were uniquely unsuited to fill. Some of these freaks and geeks were novelty acts, imagined by owners to entice fans. Others were merely dabbling in baseball, when their day jobs would inevitably involve acting, or sprinting, or playing basketball. Regardless of their credentials, these players enjoyed very short baseball careers, with very limited success, before returning to their real life's work. Like extraterrestrials, their visits were weird and largely inexplicable.

SHORT STORY OF EDDIE GAEDEL

The tale of Eddie Gaedel is forever intertwined with the story of the eccentric baseball owner Bill Veeck, an irrepressible showman who always believed baseball should be as much entertainment as it is sport. Veeck went to great lengths to pull off stunts that today would be considered bush-league or even politically

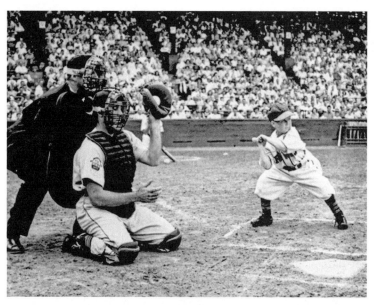

Small in stature, 3-foot-7 Eddie Gaedel was good for big laughs—and one base on balls in 1951 for St. Louis Browns owner Bill Veeck. *AP Photo*

incorrect. He continued to do so right through his tenure with the Chicago White Sox, when in 1979 a Disco Demolition Night inspired by Veeck and his son Mike turned into a disastrous riot at Comiskey Park.

There was nothing so destructive on August 19, 1951, about the plate appearance of Gaedel, a little person and midwestern vaudevillian who was all of three feet seven inches tall. There had been a James Thurber fictional story in 1941 about just such a stunt, though Veeck always insisted he drew his inspiration instead from an idea dropped by the Giants' manager John McGraw, a longtime finagler of the rules. Gaedel famously came to bat in the bottom of the first inning for Veeck's struggling St. Louis Browns, who were at the time thirty-six games behind the Yanks in the standings and desperately seeking audiences. When Gaedel pinch-hit for the leadoff man Frank Saucier in the second game of a doubleheader against the Tigers, he changed forever the way Major League Baseball conducted its own bureaucratic affairs.

Veeck would later write of Gaedel, "He was, by golly, the best darn midget who ever played big-league ball. He was also the only one." The owner went to great lengths to set up this particular event in Sportsman's Park, which he had billed as a "festival of surprises" to honor the American League's fiftieth anniversary in conjunction with Falstaff Brewery, the club's radio sponsor. While secretly signing Gaedel and fitting him into a Browns uniform with the number ⅛ on the back, Veeck made certain there was room on the active roster for this small addition. All the proper paperwork was filed with the league at the last minute, too late for close inspection. Then the contract was placed in the hands of St. Louis's manager, Zack Taylor, so that he could nimbly deflect the predictable challenge by the umpire Ed Hurley on the field. Veeck had another impish idea, too. Between games of the doubleheader, he arranged for Gaedel to pop out of a three-tiered, seven-foot papier-mâché cake on the field, never telling anyone that this same fellow would soon be batting for the Browns in the nightcap.

Gaedel himself was twenty-six years old, a mascot and model for Mercury Records who had been a former airplane riveter during World War II. He was a professional performer, a guild member. Gaedel was not, however, a baseball player by any stretch of the imagination. Years later, Saucier told the *Detroit Free Press* he had mixed feelings about being lifted in the very first inning for this novel pinch hitter. "Three thoughts went through my mind that day," Saucier said. "One, this is more like a carnival or a circus than a professional baseball game. Two, this is the greatest bit of showmanship I've ever seen. Three, this is the easiest money I'll ever make."

Gaedel walked to the plate waving three toy bats upon his introduction. Veeck instructed him to get into a low crouch and not to swing at a pitch under any circumstances. According to later accounts by the Browns' wacky owner, Veeck had measured Gaedel's strike zone under these low-crouch conditions and found it to be exactly one and a half inches high. The little player, however, did not crouch quite as low as planned when he came to the plate, a clear betrayal of faith as far as Veeck was concerned.

Nonetheless, this remained a relatively tiny strike zone, and not one that the pitcher, Bob Cain, could handle. To his great credit, Cain was amused and not visibly annoyed by this spectacle. The Tiger pitcher threw four straight balls to Gaedel, all predictably high, despite a low target from the catcher, Bob Swift, down on his knees behind the plate. Cain experimented with lobs on the last two pitches, to no avail. "I didn't know whether to throw the ball underhanded or overhanded," he told the writer Danny Peary. "I just wanted to be careful not to hit him." Having drawn his walk, Gaedel received a standing ovation from the crowd of 18,369, tipping his cap twice on the way down to first base. There, he was quickly replaced by the pinch runner Jim Delsing, who was stranded at third during a 6–2 Tiger victory. "I'm glad to have been a part of it," said George Kell, the Hall of Fame third baseman for Detroit. "We Tigers laughed it off, because we figured we were going to win." They did, but Gaedel had more than earned his $100 performer's fee. "For a minute," Gaedel said, "I felt like Babe Ruth."

Major League Baseball, humorless to a fault, was predictably outraged by Veeck's antics and moved quickly to shore up its rules. Gaedel's base on balls was at first removed from the record books, though it relented a year later when his career on-base percentage was listed as 1.000. The American League's president, Will Harridge, declared Gaedel's contract null and void the very next day after his appearance, at which point Veeck protested that Gaedel was not that much shorter than the Yankees' shortstop Phil Rizzuto. MLB denied this appeal and instituted a new policy that all new contracts would have to be immediately approved by the commissioner's office.

As for Gaedel, he continued to perform on occasion for Veeck in different roles. Ten years after he drew his walk, Veeck hired Gaedel and six other little people—the Seven Dwarfs—as vendors at Comiskey Park. This way, Veeck figured, they would not block the view of fans. Gaedel met a tragic end at age thirty-six, when he suffered a fatal heart attack after being beaten badly during a row at a Chicago bowling alley. The only former baseball player at his funeral reportedly was Bob Cain, the gallant Tiger pitcher with the gracious sense of humor. Later, Gaedel's grand-nephew Kyle Gaedele became a legitimate ballplayer, drafted in the thirty-second round of the 2008 draft by the Tampa Bay Rays. Kyle was six foot three and had a large strike zone.

ALLAN TRAVERS, ACCIDENTAL TIGER

Aloysius Joseph Travers pitched a complete game for the Tigers on May 18, 1912, giving up twenty-six hits, seven walks, and twenty-four runs, fourteen of them earned. It was his one and only appearance in the major leagues, and a very inauspicious one indeed. But that is only a tiny part of his silly, meandering tale. Travers was a replacement player of sorts, recruited only because of a strike by the Detroit Tigers over a well-earned league suspension of Ty Cobb.

The story really starts at Hilltop Park in Manhattan, where Cobb was heckled by a fan, Claude Lueker, who by all accounts called Cobb a "half-nigger." This particularly rankled Cobb, who was himself a renowned racist. Cobb hoped to have the fan tossed but could not find the New York Highlanders' owner Frank Farrell to perform the task. Lueker, it turned out, had lost one hand and also three fingers on the other hand in a printing press accident a few months earlier. Nonetheless, at the urging of his teammates, Cobb confronted Lueker and began beating him up, to the horror of spectators in the crowd who pointed out the man's disabilities. "I don't care if he has no feet," Cobb supposedly responded, continuing the one-sided fight.

The appropriately named Ban Johnson, the American League president, happened to be in attendance that day and suspended Cobb indefinitely. Though Cobb's teammates did not particularly like the star, they backed him on this particular issue and declared they would not play another game until Cobb's suspension was lifted. Johnson threatened to fine the Tigers' owner, Frank Navin, $5,000 if the Tigers did not play, so Navin demanded that his manager, Hughie Jennings, come up with a team. The Tigers were in Philly at the time, and Jennings happened to know a local Philadelphia *Bulletin* sportswriter, Joe Nolan. Jennings asked help from Nolan, who knew Travers, an assistant manager of the St. Joseph's College baseball team. Travers then recruited eight more amateur players from his North Philly neighborhood, and each was paid $25 to become sacrificial lambs. That Saturday, to start the game, the real Tigers took the field. But Cobb was ordered off by the umpires, and his teammates followed in solidarity.

The replacements then appeared, led by Travers, the twenty-year-old college junior and a violinist in the student orchestra. Travers had never pitched in an organized game in his life. His primary job with the St. Joseph's team was producing game recaps for the yearbook. Travers planned to play the outfield. But Nolan informed the players that the pitcher would be paid double, $50, and Travers decided to give it a shot.

What followed was slapstick comedy. Travers's slow curve confounded the A's hitters for a while. He later told the sportswriter Red Smith that a coach, Joe Sugden, chastised him when he attempted to throw a fastball: "Just throw your regular stuff. It ain't good enough to hit." Going into the bottom of the fifth inning, the game was surprisingly competitive, with the Tigers trailing by just 6–2. At this juncture, however, the A's decided on a different tack to deal with these odd pitches from Travers. They began to bunt the ball against the hopeless infield and scored eight runs, as attempted throws to first base flew into the stands. Philadelphia's Eddie Collins stole five bases. The A's knocked four doubles and six triples, though no homers, off Travers.

Much to his dismay, Travers became something of a local celebrity. His photograph ran the next day in a Philly newspaper with the headline "Strikebreaking Pitcher," and his mom was visited, unpleasantly, by some local union members. There was a strike of city transit workers at the time, and replacement workers, or scabs, were not considered particularly good citizens. A union called the Baseball Players Fraternity was formed in August, in good part because of this incident, and attracted a membership of 288 players—including the board members Cobb and Christy Mathewson. It lasted five years and is still considered a forerunner of today's Players Association. Cobb's suspension was reduced to five days and his fine dropped to $50. His Tiger teammates were fined $100 apiece for walking off the job. Though Navin wanted to pay those fines, Ban Johnson insisted the money come out of the players' paychecks as a lesson. Meanwhile, a public campaign by the sportswriter Grantland Rice led to new rules controlling the behavior of ballpark fans. As for Travers, he was ordained as a Catholic priest in 1926 and became dean of men at St. Joseph's. He never threw another slow curveball to a major-league hitter, and the reverend's ERA stood at 15.75 at his death in 1968. He did not, however, set the all-time record for worst single pitching performance. That distinction was held by Dave Rowe, a middling center fielder and shortstop by trade who took very occasional turns on the mound. When he did so for the Cleveland Blues in 1882, Rowe gave up thirty-five runs (twelve earned), twenty-nine hits, and seven walks. By comparison, Travers was Cy Young.

HERB WASHINGTON, DESIGNATED RUNNER

The Athletics' owner Charlie Finley always liked to think outside the batter's box, whether it was building a short home run porch back in Kansas City, designing yellow uniforms in Oakland, or limiting the number of broken bats permitted for each of his players. In 1974, he had a particularly eccentric brainstorm. Finley signed Herb Washington, a star sprinter at Michigan State and world record holder, to fill a roster spot as a designated runner. This was not an entirely new idea for Finley. During the previous six seasons, the A's had used Allan Lewis in this role, terming him the Panamanian Express. Lewis had stolen forty-four bases over that period while coming to the plate only twenty-nine times, batting .207 and only very occasionally playing left field. But Washington was projected as even more of a specialist than Lewis. His sole purpose would be to enter a game as a pinch runner and to steal bases.

There was one roadblock to all this. Washington had just signed a contract to play football with the Toronto Northmen of the World Football League. Finley offered Washington a better deal, and suddenly Washington's football career was finished.

"I think he will be responsible for the winning of at least ten games during the season," Finley said after he signed Washington. "Washington has already made the team and he hasn't even arrived in camp yet. That's how highly we think of him."

Baseball long-timers scoffed at Washington and called him Finley's Folly. It turned out they were basically right. A sprinter with no professional baseball experience was not a very good base runner. Washington was untrained in the fine arts of taking a proper lead and reading pitchers who fully understood his intentions. Appearing in 105 games over two seasons for Oakland, exclusively as a pinch runner, Washington stole 31 bases and was caught stealing 17 times—more than one-third of the

Experiment backfires: Herb Washington, Oakland's designated pinch
runner, is picked off first base by Mike Marshall of the Dodgers in
the ninth inning of Game 2 in the 1974 World Series. *AP Photo*

time—not a satisfactory rate of success. By comparison, at his
peak in 1962, Maury Wills stole 104 bases and was caught only
13 times.

Washington took up a precious roster spot on a championship club yet never batted, never played the field. The experiment unraveled most dramatically during Game 2 of the 1974
World Series. With the team trailing 3–2 in the ninth and nobody
out, the manager, Alvin Dark, brought in Washington to run for
Joe Rudi at first base. After Gene Tenace struck out, Washington
was picked off first base on an 0-1 count by Mike Marshall for
the critical second out with the pinch hitter Angel Mangual at
the plate. Marshall, oddly enough, had once taught a class in
kinesiology attended by Washington at Michigan State. "We set
him up and finished him off," the Dodger manager, Walt Alston,
said about the play. The A's lost Game 2, 3–2, their only defeat in

the Series. The moment was a humiliation for the proud Washington, who was jeered by a waiting crowd at the airport when the team returned to Oakland for Game 3. "I know Mr. Finley was disappointed," Washington said. "He hasn't spoken to me. He is innovative and this was one of his pet projects. I wanted to make him look good. I owe Mike Marshall and the Dodgers a debt. And it's a debt I will be disappointed if I don't collect. I want another chance. If Marshall makes that move again, he won't catch me."

Washington pinch-ran in two other World Series games but didn't attempt a steal. He managed to get a championship ring out of it all and to appear on a 1975 Topps baseball card with his position listed as "pinch runner," the only such designation in Topps history. He was dropped by the A's in May 1975, after entering nine successive games without so much as an attempted steal.

Finley would not give up on his theory, though. In future years, Don Hopkins, Larry Lintz, Matt Alexander, and Darrell Woodard filled the base-stealing role with varying success. Washington, meanwhile, would go on to become a broad-based community leader and successful businessman as the owner of McDonald's franchises in the Rochester, New York, area—a specialist no longer.

CHUCK CONNORS, RIFLEMAN

Baseball was very good to Chuck Connors, though Connors was never very good at professional baseball. Eventually, the sport would lead him to starring television roles in Hollywood, where he was far more successful as a tough-guy actor in fifty-eight feature films than he had been as a major leaguer.

By most standards, the strapping six-foot, five-inch Connors was a remarkable three-sport athlete who excelled at baseball, basketball, and football. Doors opened for Kevin Joseph Connors, the son of immigrants from Newfoundland, because of his physical talents. He grew up a big Dodgers fan in a working-class Brooklyn neighborhood and supposedly got his nickname from his sister because of a penchant for playing first base as a kid and his repeated yells of "Chuck it to me!" Connors received scholarships to an exclusive private high school, then to Seton Hall University. He passed on a possible career with the Chicago Bears, who had drafted him for his potential receiving talents. Following a stint in the army as a tank instructor, Connors joined the newly formed Boston Celtics of the Basketball Association of America (soon to merge into the NBA) in 1946, playing for that franchise as a forward during its first two seasons while averaging an unimpressive 4.5 points. In November of the Celts' inaugural season, Connors took what he described as "a harmless 15- or 20-foot set shot" that banged off the rim and somehow shattered a poorly installed backboard at Boston Garden, thus becoming the first of many NBA players to accomplish this quirky, prestigious feat.

Connors had been drafted back in 1940 by his favorite team, the Dodgers, and would leave in spring straight from the Celtics in order to report to a minor-league team, hoping to jump-start his baseball career. He kicked around the minors a bit, finally fulfilling a dream of playing for his boyhood favorites at age twenty-eight, in the most ephemeral fashion: Connors came to the plate once at the end of a game for the Dodgers against Philadelphia on May 1, 1949, and made an out. At that moment, he would become one of only a dozen athletes ever to play both Major League Baseball and professional basketball—along with Dave DeBusschere, Mark Hendrickson, Gene Conley, Danny Ainge, Ron Reed, Dick Groat, Steve Hamilton, Frank Baumholtz, Dick Ricketts, Cotton Nash, and Howie Schultz.

Connors was not done with baseball yet. He played sixty-six games at first base for the Chicago Cubs in 1951, batting .239

with two homers. He was soon sent back to the minors, which was the best thing that could have happened to him. The Cubs' top minor-league team in the Pacific Coast League at the time was the Los Angeles Angels. There, Connors found his stride as both a hitter and an entertainer. He was a star for these minor-league Angels, batting .321 with twenty-three homers while also conducting TV interviews for the club's local station. He'd turn cartwheels during his home run trots and recite twisted Shakespeare phrases while grumping at umpires. One such tirade from Connors: "The slings and arrows of outrageous fortune I can take, but your blindness is ridiculous!"

While playing for this team, not far from Hollywood, Connors was spotted and signed by an MGM casting director for the role of a police captain in the 1952 Spencer Tracy–Katharine Hepburn film *Pat and Mike,* a movie directed by George Cukor about a woman golfer. "They paid me 500 dollars for my week's work in that movie," Connors said, according to an article in *Movie Collector's World.* "I figured they'd made some mistake on the adding machine, but I stuck the check in my pocket and shut up. Baseball, I told myself, just lost a first baseman."

By 1958, Connors was starring in his own television show, playing another hard-edged character, Lucas McCain in *The Rifleman.* The series ran for five years and 168 episodes. McCain was a widower with a modified Winchester rifle, raising his son on a New Mexico ranch. Even during this career before the cameras, Connors tried to stay close to his first loves, baseball and the Dodgers. In 1966, when the actor had moved on to star in a second television series, *Branded,* he acted as something of a mediator in the salary negotiations between Los Angeles's general manager, Buzzie Bavasi, and the club's top pitchers, Sandy Koufax and Don Drysdale. Connors was invited to attend the press conference announcing a deal. In the photograph taken that day, he never looked happier.

DANNY AINGE AND THE WRONG DECISION

Danny Ainge was born in Eugene, Oregon, with an excess of athletic talent that left him torn in three directions—Major League Baseball being decidedly the wrong path. At his Eugene high school, Ainge became the first student athlete in history to be named first-team all-American in basketball, baseball, and football. He was impossibly excellent at every sport he attempted, yet he seemed to be best of all at basketball while leading North Eugene to two state basketball championships in 1976 and 1977.

From there Ainge would go on to star at Brigham Young University, where he famously drove the court with seven seconds left in a 1981 NCAA tournament game to knock out Notre Dame. He won several awards during his senior year, including the John R. Wooden Award given to the best college player in the nation. Unfortunately, Ainge prematurely signed a three-year, $525,000 contract with the Toronto Blue Jays to play baseball, before he truly blossomed into a star his senior year and was drafted by the Boston Celtics.

"When I signed the contract I was sure I wanted to play baseball, but it was too early," Ainge later told *Sports Illustrated.* "I should have waited until after my senior year. I never imagined I would have the kind of year that I did [24.4 points per game]. My thinking was that I was stuck in a bad situation for three years and I should try and make the most out of it. I know I told a lot of people I was going to play baseball, but there's a difference between saying, 'I have a contract to play baseball,' and 'I have a contract to play baseball but I really don't want to,' which is how I felt."

Disappointing stints followed for Ainge at second base, shortstop, third base, and all three outfield positions. Mostly, he couldn't hit. In three seasons from 1979 to 1981, Ainge batted .220 with two homers and a slugging percentage of .269 in 211 games, while striking out 128 times in 665 at-bats. For what it's worth, he did become the youngest player in franchise history to hit a home run, at twenty years and seventy-seven days. It soon became all too obvious to Ainge, however, that this baseball idea had been a terrible mistake all along, and he began searching for a loophole to get out of his contract. He wanted to join the Boston Celtics and Red Auerbach—the sage general manager who had chosen Ainge as the thirty-first player in the 1981 NBA draft, despite the player's contractual obligation with the Blue Jays.

"As far as I'm concerned, I'm not a part of the Toronto Blue Jays," Ainge announced. "I'm going home to Utah to get in shape for basketball. I'm retired from baseball." The Blue Jays did not appreciate what they considered illegal tampering by Auerbach and took the case to court. A jury found Ainge still obligated to the Jays, who were seeking $1 million for his rights. Eventually, the Celtics bought out Ainge's contract, and he went on to play 1,042 games over fourteen years in the NBA, averaging 11.4 points and four assists while earning $8.4 million, playing in an All-Star Game, and winning two championships in Boston. Ainge would coach the Phoenix Suns and later become general manager and president of basketball operations for the Celtics. In Boston, he engineered a forty-two-game turnaround in 2007–2008 and another title—at the Garden, not at Fenway.

DAVE DeBUSSCHERE AND ALL THAT WASTED TALENT

The trouble with Dave DeBusschere wasn't that he couldn't pitch. It was that he played basketball too well. And because of that, a potentially fine career on the mound was short-circuited just so he could go on to become a Hall of Fame NBA player and win a couple of fabled championships with the New York Knicks.

DeBusschere had excelled as both a pitcher and a hoops star at Austin Catholic High School and then with his hometown

college the University of Detroit. He was so good in college the
school named a lounge after him—and DeBusschere didn't
have to donate a single penny. An ambitious six-foot, six-inch
physical specimen, DeBusschere signed contracts in 1962 with

both the Chicago White Sox
and the Detroit Pistons. The
balancing act was difficult,
but it could be done. He was
thrown immediately into the
big shows in two sports. With
the contending White Sox
that first season, DeBusschere
was mostly brought in as a
mop-up man to finish one-
sided games. He fared well,
but after getting knocked
around by the Twins during
one appearance in mid-June,
he was sent to the minors for
three months. There, he went
10-1 with a 2.49 ERA and

Dave DeBusschere had a 2.90 ERA
in two seasons with the White Sox
before he wasted his baseball talent
winning NBA titles with the Knicks.
AP Photo

earned a White Sox recall. Come the end of September, still only
twenty-one years old, DeBusschere donned a Pistons' uniform
to average 12.7 points and 8.7 rebounds.

In 1963, DeBusschere appeared in twenty-four games for the
White Sox, starting ten of them. Finishing the season strong, he
threw a six-hit, complete-game shutout against Cleveland on
August 13. In thirty-six games over two seasons in the majors,
DeBusschere would have a 2.90 ERA. Over three seasons in
the minors, he went 40-21. Unfortunately, the White Sox had
one of the best rotations in baseball, while the dreadful Pis-
tons pressured him to commit to basketball—a sport in which
DeBusschere clearly shined as both a scorer and a rebounder.
One day, the Pistons' executive manager, Don Wattrick, invited

DeBusschere to breakfast and asked him what he thought about player-coaches.

"They can do the job," DeBusschere said.

"What about you?" asked Wattrick.

"Sure," DeBusschere said. And with that, essentially, a baseball career was snuffed out. It was tough enough playing two professional sports. Then, at age twenty-four, DeBusschere had been hired to coach one of them, too—in his hometown, with friends, family, and fans watching his every step and misstep. Suddenly he was wearing three hats, not just two. "It was an impossible job, trying to play and coach at the same time, especially when most of the players are older than you are," DeBusschere said about his three-year tenure as NBA player-coach. He also wasn't thrilled with his progress within the White Sox organization. He quit baseball in 1965, never looking back.

DeBusschere's destiny, of course, lay in New York. He was traded to the Knicks on December 19, 1968, for Walt Bellamy and Howard Komives. Two years later, teamed with Willis Reed and Bill Bradley in the frontcourt, DeBusschere helped the Knicks win their first championship in twenty-four years. He would later become general manager of the New York Nets, commissioner of the American Basketball Association, and then GM of the Knicks. Knicks fans remember with considerable delight the sight of DeBusschere pounding the table gleefully after his team won the rights to draft Patrick Ewing in the 1985 draft lottery. All that, however, had nothing to do with his fastball.

BOTTOM TEN

1   **EDDIE GAEDEL**   Size matters, when it comes to the strike zone.

2   **ALLAN TRAVERS**   Violinist, man of the cloth, (onetime) starting pitcher for the Tigers.

3   **HERB WASHINGTON**   Fleetness of foot didn't seem to help his base running.

4   **CHUCK CONNORS**   He would play more successfully in front of Hollywood cameras.

5   **DANNY AINGE**   Picked the wrong sport, but was smart enough to get out.

6   **BO JACKSON**   Even during his one All-Star season, he struck out 172 times in 515 at-bats to lead the league.

7   **ALLAN LEWIS**   "The Panamanian Express," another Charlie Finley experiment in designated base running.

8   **DEION SANDERS**   After his first three awful seasons, turned out not quite as terrible as people thought he'd be.

9   **DAVE DeBUSSCHERE**   Could have picked any sport. Baseball's loss.

10   **DOCK ELLIS**   Legitimate pitcher, yes, but more the cult hero after throwing a no-hitter on acid.

8 | BONEHEAD
The Greatest Goats of All Time

SEVERAL PLAYERS HAVE enjoyed solid or even commendable careers, only to have everything crash down around them because of one botched event. This sort of thing may occur at the worst possible moment, with a pennant race or a title at stake. It can happen at the plate, on the base paths, on the mound, or in the field. And then there is no recovering from the incident. The one-blunder wonder is indelibly stained by his bungle, even if he wins twenty games or hits .300 in each of his next seven seasons.

Maybe it's mere coincidence, but all of the players mentioned in this chapter became undone in a game involving one or two teams in New York, Boston, or Chicago, all of them big baseball towns. That made for brighter spotlights and more lingering memories. Unpleasant memories, at that.

BILL BUCKNER AND HIS WICKETS

If you watch the error on YouTube, in grainy color, the thing that jumps out is just how quickly Bill Buckner comprehends the consequences of his famous blunder. When Mookie Wilson's

Bill Buckner watches Mookie Wilson's grounder go through his legs in Game 6 of the 1986 World Series. For Red Sox fans, the rest is misery. *Stan Grossfeld*/The Boston Globe *via Getty Images*

slow-rolling grounder down the line somehow eludes Buckner's glove and seeps between his legs, the first baseman doesn't even bother to chase the ball into short right-center field. He simply stops and stares emotionlessly in the general direction of the infield, where Ray Knight is rounding third and heading home for the run in the tenth inning that would win Game 6 of the 1986 World Series for the Mets—who would then clinch the Series in seven games. "Little roller up along first," Vin Scully called it on NBC. "Behind the bag. It gets through Buckner!"

In an instant, an antihero was made, and a formidable baseball reputation all but wrecked. In fairness, Buckner had a career over twenty-two seasons that produced close to Hall of Fame numbers, with 2,715 hits and a batting title (at .324) in 1980 with the Chicago Cubs. Even over those good years, Buckner endured plenty of hardships. He lost another World Series in 1974 with the Dodgers. He limped for nearly an entire season with the Cubs, playing on a staph-infected ankle. He was ripped in 1979 by the outgoing Chicago manager, Herman Franks, who called him selfish and said of Buckner, "What I found out, after being around him for a while, is that he's nuts."

So yes, Buckner took his lumps along the way, but nothing like what happened in Shea Stadium. That Game 6 had many possible endings that might have spared Buckner the torment. In Games 1, 2, and 5, Boston's manager, John McNamara, removed Buckner for defensive purposes when the Red Sox held leads. Yet for some reason, in Game 6, after Boston moved ahead by two runs in the top of the tenth, McNamara did not bring in Dave Stapleton as a replacement this time. It wasn't as if Buckner's bat were desperately needed. He was slumping, batting .143 in the Series and 0 for 5 in the game. Then the Red Sox bullpen imploded. Calvin Schiraldi yielded three two-out singles, and Bob Stanley threw a wild pitch. A game that should have been won was already tied, even before Buckner's misplay. Nonetheless, the fallout from the error was both immediate and long-term. The Red Sox hadn't won a title since dumping Babe Ruth on the Yankees, and this collapse just fed into the whole city's persecution complex.

Buckner came to epitomize the franchise's failings. He was traded to the Angels midway through the next season, leaving town until things cooled off. By the time he was brought back to the Red Sox in 1990 as a free agent at the end of his career, tempers had abated, and he had become something of a novelty item. The Fenway fans gave him a standing ovation at the home opener, before he retired in June. Buckner hosted his own Boston radio talk show in the early 1990s, though he was notably unenthusiastic (when this author appeared as a guest on one broadcast, Buckner said before the airing, "Let's just get this over with"). On April 8, 2008, Buckner was invited back to Fenway again to throw out the first pitch and again received a heartfelt, four-minute ovation. By then, the Red Sox had won the 2004 and 2007 World Series. The meltdown in 1986 was a distant, almost affectionate memory. "I really had to forgive, not the fans of Boston, per se, but I would have to say in my heart I had to forgive the media for what they put me and my family through," Buckner said to reporters at that Opening Day. "So, you know, I've done that and I'm over that."

He was done with it, yet still able to cash in a bit. Buckner appeared on Larry David's HBO comedy, *Curb Your Enthusiasm*, where he redeemed himself by neatly catching a baby thrown from a blazing apartment building. Charlie Sheen, of all people, bought the "Buckner Ball" in 1992 for $93,000 at an auction, before it was sold to the songwriter Seth Swirsky. Swirsky kindly renamed his memento the "Mookie Ball." Everyone still knew whose legs it squirmed through.

FRED MERKLE AND HIS BONER

Fred Merkle stole an impressive 272 bases during a successful sixteen-year career in the majors, yet forever will be remembered as the man who made the worst base-running mistake in history. After committing his unfortunate mental slipup, Merkle went through life with the nickname Bonehead, a moniker he earned at the fresh-faced age of nineteen, as the youngest player in the National League with the New York Giants. The shame is that poor Merkle shouldn't even have been in the game at the Polo Grounds that caused him such eternal misery and that he might well have been a hero if not for a series of absurd events.

It all began for Merkle on the morning of September 23, 1908, when the team's regular first baseman, Fred Tenney, informed the manager, John McGraw, he couldn't play in the big game

against the Cubs because of a sore back. In this era, position players were generally afforded no days off. But McGraw reluctantly
called on the backup, Merkle, at first base, the kid's first career
start. The Giants and the Cubs were in a virtual tie for first place,

only percentage points apart
with a few games left to play.
The score was tied, 1–1, and
there were two outs in the
ninth when Merkle singled
Moose McCormick over to
third base, a great success.
The Giants' shortstop, Al
Bridwell, then singled to center, knocking home McCor-
mick for what appeared to
be a walk-off victory. Fans
rushed onto the field, understandably   believing   the
Giants had taken over first
place. But Merkle had gal-
loped in celebration toward
the   dugout   without   ever

Fred Merkle returns to get a tour
of the Polo Grounds, site of his
boneheaded base-running blunder
back in 1908. *AP Photos*

bothering to touch second base. Johnny Evers, the Cubs' sharp
second baseman, noticed this oversight and called for the ball
from the center fielder, Solly Hofman.

What happened to the baseball at this juncture remains open
to debate. According to some accounts, Joe McGinnity, a Giants
pitcher who was coaching first, intercepted the relay and hurled
the ball into the crowd. But Evers somehow retrieved it or got
another one—or by one account was thrown the ball by his
poetic infield mate, the shortstop Joe Tinker. In any case, the
umpires ruled Merkle out on a force play at second base, and
the run was disallowed. Fans stormed after the home plate

umpire, Henry O'Day, who required considerable police protection. O'Day wrote a letter to the National League commissioner, Harry Pulliam, explaining, "I did not ask to have the field cleared, as it was too dark to continue play." After an appeals process, Pulliam ruled in favor of the Cubs and forced a replay of the whole game—which the Cubs won in October, breaking a first-place tie with the Giants. This allowed Chicago to capture the pennant by one game on their way to their last World Series title in . . . forever.

The reaction to all this was not pretty in New York, which always takes its baseball seriously. *The New York Times* termed Merkle's play "censurable stupidity" and wrote, "His unusual conduct in the final inning of a great game perhaps deprived New York of a victory that would have been unquestionable had he not committed a breach in baseball play."

Merkle remained a favorite player of the Giants' manager, John McGraw, who admired his aggression on the base paths. Merkle rewarded his manager by batting .309 in 1912. But then bad karma struck again that season in the World Series against Boston. Tris Speaker's foul pop dropped between pitcher Christy Mathewson, catcher Chief Meyers, and Merkle. As the first baseman, Merkle arguably should have made the play. Given a second life, Speaker started the winning rally for the Red Sox with a hit off Mathewson. Merkle retired in 1926, doomed by his very nickname to live in infamy. He stayed far away from the game, avoiding all baseball-related ceremonies and gatherings. But then, in 1950, six years before his death, Merkle appeared at a Giants Old Timers Day game. He received a standing ovation in the Polo Grounds, proof that even New Yorkers place a statute of limitations on bungling.

RALPH BRANCA AND THE FASTBALL
HE SHOULDN'T HAVE THROWN

Ralph Branca might easily have become bitter or just plain worn-out. Yet for decades after he threw the pitch to Bobby Thomson that became the "shot heard 'round the world," Branca would willingly, sportingly speak on the subject of that 1951 playoff game. Branca somehow managed to maintain a healthy self-image and a sense of humor on the subject. And when Thomson died in 2010, Branca attended the funeral, "to say goodbye to a good friend."

It is a shame if such a man, and such a respectable pitcher, should be defined by one fastball. Branca was a three-time All-Star who won twenty-one games in 1947, when he had a 2.67 ERA and 148 strikeouts. Over his twelve-year career, he was 88-68 with a 3.79 ERA and might have amassed a more impressive mark if back problems hadn't contributed to an early retirement in 1956 at age thirty.

Ralph Branca and Bobby Thomson remained friends long after the Shot Heard 'Round the World—which was very nice of Branca, all things considered. *New York* Daily News

That is all well and good, but eventually we come to Branca on the mound in the Polo Grounds for the Brooklyn Dodgers and Thomson at bat for the New York Giants on October 3, 1951, in the third and deciding playoff game for the National League pennant. The Giants had come back from a thirteen-and-a-half-game deficit during the regular season with the aid of a sixteen-

Ralph Branca delivers his fastball to Bobby Thomson in 1951,
and the Giants win the pennant, win the pennant,
win the pennant . . . *AP Photo*

game winning streak, and now were coming back again in this
game. Branca was summoned from the bullpen in the ninth
inning instead of a second option, Carl Erskine. Clyde Sukeforth,
a Dodgers' coach, told the manager, Charlie Dressen, that Erskine was throwing curveballs into the dirt during warm-ups, so
Dressen called on Branca instead to relieve Don Newcombe—
even though Branca was working on only one day's rest and
Thomson had already homered off him in Game 1. The Dodgers
led, 4–2, with runners at second and third and one out. First base
was open. The rookie Willie Mays was on deck. Branca threw
two fastballs to Thomson. Thomson lined the second one for a
three-run walk-off homer to left. The radio commentator Russ
Hodges screamed four times, "The Giants win the pennant!"
The New York baseball landscape was never the same.

Branca later became aware that the Giants were stealing his
catcher's signs by using a telescope from the center field stands.

The story was broken by *The Wall Street Journal* in 2001 and included a confession by Sal Yvars, the Giants' catcher. Yvars confirmed the story to Branca. "He said, 'I gave him the pitch,'" Branca said. Thomson denied getting tipped off about the fastball on the actual home run pitch while admitting to receiving tips on some of Branca's other pitches. Branca never confronted his friend Thomson on the matter. "I think he didn't want to demean what he did," Branca said after Thomson's death. "But in my mind, I think he would have been a bigger man if he admitted it."

In any case, the revelations did little or nothing to change the conventional narrative. Thomson was the hero, Branca the goat. "People don't want to change history," Branca told the *Los Angeles Times*. "Thomson's a good guy, was humble, never lorded it over me, had decent values, good family man, good provider, good husband. I know what it was, I know how I pitched. Even though I get blamed for it, I'm not the guy who lost the pennant."

It is easy to say Branca's career was never the same. It wasn't. But his back injury during the next spring training was really the culprit. He struggled for two seasons in Brooklyn, then was picked off waivers by the Tigers in 1953, later signing as a free agent with the Yankees in 1954. After a year in the Giants' minor-league system, Branca was given his last shot back with the Dodgers in 1956. He appeared in one final game on September 7, striking out two batters and allowing no runs in two innings of impressive mop-up duty during a 6–2 loss to—whom else?—the New York Giants.

STEVE BARTMAN'S FOUL PLAY

The Chicago Cubs were five outs away from their first pennant in fifty-eight years on October 14, 2003, leading the Florida Marlins 3–2 in the National League Championship Series and 3–0 in the eighth inning of Game 6. Luis Castillo lofted a catchable foul fly down the left field line at Wrigley Field, where the committed Cubs fan Steve Bartman made a play for it in the front row (for the record, he was sitting in section 4, row 8, seat 113, now a tourist stop). Bartman deflected the baseball that had seemed destined for the glove of the left fielder, Moises Alou. When the ball dropped, Alou threw his glove to the ground, admonishing Bartman and other spectators, appealing to the umpire Mike Everitt for an interference call. Everitt refused to do so, ruling the ball had passed the plane of the wall into the stands.

Mark Prior was pitching a three-hit shutout at the time, but suddenly everything fell apart. Castillo walked, Iván Rodríguez singled, Chicago shortstop Alex González mishandled a potential double-play grounder from Miguel Cabrera, and Derrek Lee doubled. The reliever Kyle Farnsworth had no better luck, and eventually the Marlins batted around for eight runs in the inning. Bartman remained in his seat through this entire debacle, occasionally featured on television and soon identified on Internet message boards. With his Cubs cap, glasses, and earphones, Bartman was an unassuming villain, a twenty-six-year-old business consultant who lived with his parents and helped coach baseball basics to local kids. He was eventually led out of Wrigley Field by security guards while other fans—who likely would have reached for the same foul ball—pelted Bartman with beer, debris, and insults.

The Marlins would then come back again in Game 7 for a 9–6 victory, making Bartman even more of a target, the most hated man in all of the North Side of Chicago. Angry fans called for his head, while TV satellite trucks parked in front of his parents' home. Half jokingly, Illinois's governor, Rod Blagojevich—who would soon have his own, more serious legal problems—suggested Bartman join a witness protection program. Instead, Bartman simply released a statement of apology, with an explanation.

"I'm truly sorry from the bottom of this Cubs fan's broken heart," Bartman stated. "I had my eyes glued on the approaching ball the entire time and was so caught up in the moment that I did not even see Moises Alou, much less that he may have had a play." Bartman donated all money to charity that was sent to him from mischievous Marlins fans. The baseball itself was eventually sold to Harry Caray's Restaurant Group and was exploded during a public demonstration in February 2004. Pieces of the ball were boiled, and the steam was used as an ingredient in a tomato sauce.

After his apology, Bartman quite effectively vanished from public life. He deflected questions from stalking reporters. He never accepted invitations to talk shows or autograph conventions, and he reportedly turned down a six-figure offer to appear in a Super Bowl ad.

"If he ever chooses to speak publicly, it will be in a time and place and medium of his choice, not one that has been imposed on him by others," his friend Frank Murtha, an attorney, told the *Chicago Tribune* in 2011. "That's not to say he will do that. At this point, he has no immediate plans for discussion. He is happy, because that's who he is."

As for Alou, he at least once graciously suggested that he might not even have caught the foul ball. "It's time to forgive the guy and move on," Alou said.

DONNIE MOORE AND THE FORKBALL THAT DIDN'T DIP

Unlike Branca, who came to terms over time with his goat's horns, Donnie Moore devolved into a forlorn, tragic figure because of one pitch to Dave Henderson of the Red Sox in the 1986 American League Championship Series. Moore had grown accustomed to much happier endings. In his thirteen-year career, the right-handed reliever would save eighty-nine games with a 3.67 ERA. In 1985, when he posted a 1.92 ERA with thirty-one saves, Moore was an All-Star while finishing seventh in Cy Young voting and sixth in balloting for the league's Most Valuable Player. His 1986 season was not as strong because of back problems, but there was no way to predict the downfall that would follow in Game 5, with the California Angels ahead three games to one and almost certain to reach their first World Series in history before the home fans.

The Angels led, 5–2, heading into the top of the ninth inning. Television camera crews scurried into the California clubhouse to record the impending celebration. Don Baylor's two-run shot off Mike Witt—who would somehow escape the wrath of local fans—suddenly made it a tight, one-run game. With two outs and nobody on, Gary Lucas came in from the pen and plunked Rich Gedman with a pitch. Gene Mauch, the perpetually star-crossed manager, signaled for Moore, who had successfully saved Game 3. Moore went to a 2-2 count on Henderson before throwing a hanging forkball. Henderson had appeared over-matched in the at-bat, barely hanging in there by fouling off pitches and hoping for a mistake. He finally got one.

"I made a bad pitch," Moore said. "Usually, my ball dips. That ball didn't dip. You make bad pitches, you lose games. This one is going to follow me around for a while."

The Angels tied the game in the bottom of the ninth and should have won it right then, with bases loaded and one out. Doug DeCinces and Bobby Grich both failed to score the runner from third, and the game dragged on. Moore gave the Angels another chance to win by throwing a scoreless tenth inning, when Jim Rice grounded into a double play. Almost cruelly, Mauch kept Moore in the game for the eleventh inning, when Henderson scored Baylor with a sacrifice fly for the winning run. The Red Sox won, 7–6. The Angels then completely collapsed and dropped the final two games at Fenway, 10–4 and 8–1. "You could feel it," DeCinces would say later about Game 5. "All of a sudden everything was gone."

It was worst for Moore, who became an easy target in Anaheim. He was jeered mercilessly over his next two seasons there, as his aging arm and back problems sabotaged his stats. He saved only nine more games in forty-one appearances after that ALCS, while his ERA ballooned to 4.91 in his final season, 1988. Moore had earned $3 million over his final three seasons with the Angels, but money was not enough to salve the wounds of 1986. After he was cut by Kansas City in June 1989—without a single major-league appearance for the Royals—Moore returned home to Anaheim, miserable. His career was in shambles. His marriage was falling apart. Moore shot his wife, Tonya, three times, then committed suicide. His wife survived the attack. "When he was cut by Kansas City, he'd really been depressed about that," said his daughter, Demetria. "I mean, here he is, the high-life career, then all of a sudden it's gone. He comes back home, and the marriage, the family, is all destroyed. I mean, what does he have left?"

In Moore's case, not enough.

LUIS CASTILLO AND THE DROPPED POP

Luis Castillo was a three-time Gold Glove winner and All-Star earlier in his career, but by 2009 he was already a symbol of futility on the New York Mets and the target of considerable fan rage. The second baseman had been signed by Omar Minaya to an extravagant four-year, $25 million contract in 2007, then had a horrid 2008 season at the plate and in the field while battling injuries.

All of this was mere prelude, however, to what would happen on June 12, 2009, when the Mets faced their cross-borough rivals, the Yankees. The Mets had not yet come to understand they were a terrible team, and they were sitting in second place with a respectable 31-27 record when they visited the Bronx for an emotionally charged series. Then, in the opener, all looked wonderful after David Wright's eighth-inning double off the Yankees' closer, Mariano Rivera, gave the Mets an 8–7 lead. The reliever

Francisco Rodríguez allowed a couple of Yanks to reach base, but then Alex Rodríguez hit a simple pop-up behind first base for what would surely be the third and final out.

Somehow, it wasn't. While Rodríguez slammed his bat in disgust, Castillo drifted toward the foul line, correctly calculating the arc. Incredibly, he allowed the ball to drop out of his glove. He was not impeded by a teammate or distracted by a fan. This was an inexcusable Little League error, and the Yankees proved heartless opportunists. Derek Jeter scored

Luis Castillo drops an easy pop-up to second base off the bat of Alex Rodríguez and the Yankees beat the Mets, as usual, in a 2009 game. *Noah K. Murray*/The Star Ledger

from second, and Mark Teixeira, ever the hustler, scored from first base for the walk-off victory, 9–8.

"As soon as I slid in, I hugged Jete and I said, 'What just happened?'" Teixeira said. "Because I couldn't believe it."

Teixeira was lauded for his heads-up base running, while poor Castillo was vilified further by Mets fans for what was his fifth error of the season. "I feel bad. I feel so bad," Castillo said. "The ball was moving a little bit." It wasn't as if the other Mets had been playing crisp baseball. Earlier in the season, they lost a game to Florida when the outfielder Daniel Murphy dropped a fly ball off Cody Ross's bat. They'd lost another one when Ryan Church missed third base while heading toward home for the potential winning run against the Dodgers. But this was the Subway Series, and Castillo was already a scapegoat before the latest mistake. "We feel like we just stole one," Jeter said.

Castillo managed to get his act together for the rest of the season, rallying to bat .302. But the Mets never seemed to recover from the psychological blow. "We'll have to fight through this," Jerry Manuel said. "This is definitely a tremendous test for us." The Mets failed the exam. By July, they were under .500, and they would finish the season in fourth place, at 70-92. Castillo endured one more season with the Mets, despite a rising clamor in the city for his exit. After batting just .235 in 2010, he was cut by the new general manager, Sandy Alderson, on March 18, 2011. The Mets were still on the hook for $6 million on Castillo's pact and owned no obvious successor at second base. Alderson all but admitted, in general manager–ese, that his decision was based in part on Castillo's unpopularity in New York.

"I don't think there's any question there is some linkage between his situation and a perception of the Mets that has existed to this point," Alderson said. "That's something that was taken into account. At some point you have to make an organizational decision, and it goes beyond just an ability to play and to not play. Those things are relevant, and you try not to make them so controlling that it dictates the final decision under any circumstances. But realistically, it's a factor."

Nobody rued the decision, and one New York tabloid headline read END OF AN ERROR.

BOTTOM TEN

1.	**BILL BUCKNER**	Through the legs and down the line.
2	**FRED MERKLE**	Just touch the bag, stupid.
3	**RALPH BRANCA**	The Dodgers lose the pennant! The Dodgers lose the pennant!
4	**STEVE BARTMAN**	Redefined the term "long-suffering Cubs fan."
5	**MICKEY OWEN**	Brooklyn Dodgers' catcher allowed a passed ball on a called third strike that would have knotted the 1941 World Series at two games apiece against the Yankees. Guess what happened next.
6	**FRED SNODGRASS**	New York Giants' center fielder dropped a tenth-inning pop fly from Clyde Engle in the 1912 World Series that handed the Red Sox the title.
7	**DONNIE MOORE**	Tragic tale of a hanging forkball.
8	**LUIS CASTILLO**	If only it hadn't been against the Yankees.
9	**WILLIE DAVIS**	Committed three errors—two fielding, one throwing—during two successive plays in Game 2 of the 1966 World Series.
10	**HERB WASHINGTON**	Qualifies here for a second category, by getting picked off in Game 2 of the 1974 World Series.

9 | ANYONE SEEN MY MITT?
The Worst Teammates Ever

IF YOU'RE GOING to be a bastard to your fellow man, it helps to be Ty Cobb, Roger Hornsby, or Barry Bonds. Batting .420 for a season (Cobb), driving in 152 runs (Hornsby), or knocking 762 homers over a career (Bonds) is a very good reason for teammates to put up with your high maintenance, with your temper tantrums, and with your self-involved antics. Cobb could utter horrible, racist things or beat up a fan, and most everyone would look the other way. Hornsby wrestled with gambling debts and treated fellow players like the inferiors they were. Bonds traveled with an entourage and wanted little to do with teammates or the media. Then he'd smack another homer, the fans would cheer, and the Giants would smile through gritted teeth.

If you're flawed or downright lousy, however, nobody wants to deal with such heavy lifting in the clubhouse. Here are some players who drove everyone crazy. Some of them were quite good. Just not worth the nuisance factor.

JIMMY PIERSALL AND HIS DEMONS

Jimmy Piersall was a solid center fielder for much of his seven-teen years in the major leagues with five different teams, but not many baseball people wanted to put up with his uncontrolled antics. Piersall's legacy had little to do with 1,604 hits, two All-Star seasons, or two Gold Glove Awards. He became a cultural figure of note because of nasty fights with Billy Martin, umpires, fans, and manic depression—rendered even more famous by his own writings and a Hollywood movie based on his book *Fear Strikes Out.* Casey Stengel, no psychiatrist, once said of Piersall, "He's great, but you have to play him in a cage."

Piersall, born in 1929, was a three-sport star in Waterbury, Connecticut, a local legend who helped his high school capture the New England basketball championship. His father, John, a former semipro baseball player, was a house painter, while his mother, Mary, suffered from mental illness and was frequently sent off to a sanitarium. "If my father was preparing supper when I got home, it wouldn't be necessary for us to exchange a word," Piersall said. "I knew that meant my mother had gone away again." His dad pushed him extremely hard in all his ath-letic ventures, which may have contributed to Jimmy's problems later.

Piersall signed a contract with the Red Sox in 1948 and was called up to Boston in 1950 at the tender and unready age of twenty. He was a decent hitter and an outstanding fielder with range and a great arm. But by 1952, Piersall was causing raised eyebrows among teammates, creating real problems. He got into a fight with Martin before a game against the Yanks, then scrapped with a teammate, Mickey McDermott. He imitated the gaits of other Red Sox players as he ran off the field. He experi-mented with a backward home run trot. He also reportedly spanked the four-year-old son of another Red Sox teammate,

Vern Stephens, in the clubhouse. Piersall denied this incident in his book. "I know I did a lot of unusual things during this period," he wrote, "but I'm positive that I never spanked either Stephens's or anyone else's child. I might have—and probably

Jimmy Piersall was never easy on himself, teammates, or umpires. This time, he's going after the ump. *AP Photo/Frank C. Curtin*

did—give him a little pat on the flank, but I suppose I'll never be able to prove it." He was sent down in June to the minor-league team the Birmingham Barons, which was a great disappointment to Boston fans and reporters who had come to enjoy his antics. "Piersall's attitude was detrimental to this club," the Red Sox manager, Lou Boudreau, declared. The general manager, Joe Cronin, added, "Apparently, everyone on this club is against him."

Piersall swore to his wife, "No more clowning. I've got to behave myself. I've got to get back to Boston." But matters only deteriorated in Birmingham, even by Piersall's accounts. After an argument with an umpire, he wrote, "I pulled a water pistol out of my pocket, squirted the plate with it and said, 'Now maybe you can see it.'" He drew another ejection for that, his fourth since arriving in Birmingham. Piersall sat in the stands and continued to heckle the umpire, drawing a suspension. Soon, he admitted to a problem and sought psychiatric help at Westborough State Hospital.

Piersall returned to the Red Sox in 1953, knocking six hits in a single game. By 1954, he was moved to center field and considered one of the best defensive players ever in the game—despite hurting his arm during an informal throwing contest with Willie Mays. Stengel compared him favorably, even, to Joe DiMaggio. But the crazy incidents never stopped, and when his movie opened in 1957, he became even more of a novelty act. Traded to the Indians, he pulled another water pistol out of his pocket and shot an umpire. He went after hecklers in the Yankee Stadium bleachers. He threw a baseball at the scoreboard at Comiskey Park when it shot fireworks following a White Sox homer. Eventually, in 1963, he ended up playing for Stengel and the Mets, who gave up Gil Hodges for him in a trade with Washington. After hitting his hundredth career homer on June 23, 1963, Piersall ran the bases backward. Five weeks after that incident, Stengel released him. Piersall hooked on for a five-year stint with the Angels, then later went into broadcasting and steadied himself on prescribed medication.

"Probably the best thing that ever happened to me was going nuts," Piersall would say. "Whoever heard of Jimmy Piersall until that happened?"

RUBÉN RIVERA, MITT THIEF

It's difficult to assign Rubén Rivera a specific category, because he was truly awful in so many ways. But when you're the cousin of a future Hall of Famer, Mariano Rivera, a certain level of dignity and success is expected. Unfortunately, that baseball DNA did not transfer. Rivera somehow survived despite his many flaws for nine years with five teams in the major leagues, on the strength of his arm and glove in center field. The Panamanian certainly couldn't hit. Rivera batted below .210 during six of his seasons and finished with a career batting average of .216. He was a horrid base runner whose exploits have become YouTube classics. But those facts hardly begin to describe the mischief that this man wrought wherever he practiced his craft. Rivera developed a reputation as a carouser off the field and a wild card whenever he stepped inside the ballpark.

His most famous misstep occurred during spring training of 2002 in Tampa after he had re-signed with the Yankees. Rivera had come up through the Yankees' system as a top prospect in the 1990s, after he was recommended as a seventeen-year-old by another Yankee prospect, his cousin Mariano. In 2002, Rubén was still familiar to coaches, and the club required some outfield insurance behind the aging Bernie Williams. Brian Cashman signed Rivera as a free agent on Valentine's Day 2002. He was released just twenty-five days later, after he stole one of Derek Jeter's black Rawlings gloves from the clubhouse, sold it for $2,500 to a memorabilia dealer, then reacquired the glove and gave it back to Jeter with an apology. By releasing him, the Yanks rescued nearly $1 million in salary and the morale of players. "The clubhouse is a special place," Joe Torre, the manager, said after Rivera was dumped. "We feel it's our sanctuary. I'd like to believe we commit to each other and trust each other. It's a big part of what we do. Trust is very important if you're expected to make a commitment. Anything that threatens that type of balance we have is a negative."

That should have been that for Rivera, but he was somehow picked up by Texas and then by the San Francisco Giants for the 2003 season. There, at Pac Bell Park, he became known for what was described on air at the time by the announcer Jon Miller as "the worst base running in the history of the game." This was no exaggeration. The nonsensical play occurred in May 2003 when Rivera was playing for the Giants in a game tied 2–2 in the bottom of the ninth inning. Because Rivera had some speed, the manager, Felipe Alou, sent him to pinch-run for Andrés Galarraga, representing the potential winning run at first base. Marquis Grissom then hit a high fly ball to right that was misjudged by the Arizona outfielder David Dellucci, who dropped it for an error. Rivera had run past second base and somehow thought that Dellucci had caught the ball. Already past second base, Rivera headed back toward first, then realized the ball hadn't been caught and headed back toward third. But this time he missed second base and had to return to touch the bag. For reasons known only to Rivera, he then decided to go for third base. The relay arrived in time to nail him, but the ball skipped away from Alex Cintrón, the Arizona third baseman. Rivera bumped into Cintrón and foolishly pushed his luck yet again, heading for home. The D-Back shortstop, Tony Womack, retrieved the ball and threw out Rivera by a good five feet at the plate. "I don't know if I can sleep tonight," Rivera said afterward. "In all my career, it's the first time it's happened. I know it's going to be on the highlights. I'm not sad, but I am sad that I tried to score and it didn't happen. Everything was so quick, I didn't have time to think."

Rivera wouldn't quit trying. He hooked on with a White Sox farm club, the Triple-A Charlotte Knights, and batted only .239 in 2006. He then headed for the Piratas of the Mexican League, where the bases no doubt proved just as befuddling.

JOHN ROCKER, BIG MOUTH

Rarely has a mean mouth sabotaged a career with the alacrity and force of John Rocker's tongue. In 1999 and 2000, Rocker was one of the most fearsome, effective young closers in baseball for Atlanta with sixty-two saves to go along with ERAs of 2.49 and 2.89. But he had already laid the groundwork for his own demise in a profile piece published by *Sports Illustrated* during the winter between those two seasons. During interview sessions with the reporter Jeff Pearlman, the Statesboro, Georgia, lefty flashed his red neck with pride while lashing out at several ethnic groups—particularly at the melting pot known as New York, where the Mets played.

Was there ever a more obnoxious player than John Rocker? You be the judge. *AP Photo/Ric Feld*

Rocker was coming off an impressive National League Championship Series against the Mets in which he appeared in all six games and made a point of sneering at fans in Shea Stadium after his save in Game 3. Pearlman asked Rocker if he would ever consider pitching in New York. What followed was a disturbing xenophobic, homophobic tirade.

"I'd retire first," Rocker said. "It's the most hectic, nerve-racking city. Imagine having to take the 7 Train to the ballpark looking like you're riding through Beirut next to some kid with purple hair, next to some queer with AIDS, right next to some dude who just got out of jail for the fourth time, right next to some 20-year-old mom with four kids. It's depressing. . . . The biggest thing I don't like about New York are the foreigners. You can walk an entire block in Times Square and not hear anybody speaking English. Asians and Koreans and Vietnamese and Indians and Russians and Spanish people and everything up there. How the hell did they get in this country?"

Rocker also called Mets fans "degenerates" and commented, "Nowhere else in the country do people spit at you, throw bottles at you, throw quarters at you, throw batteries at you and say, 'Hey, I did your mother last night—she's a whore.'"

For this self-destructive diatribe, Rocker was suspended twenty-eight games—a penalty later reduced to fourteen games. He apologized, sort of. He went on the Braves' sister station, TBS, and said, "Hindsight being twenty-twenty, I would've loved to have missed my meeting with the *Sports Illustrated* reporter and I never would've had to deal with the whole situation." He attended a sensitivity training session, though Rocker later revealed he left after only fifteen minutes, "and it satisfied the powers that be."

He wasn't nearly finished with the nonsense. According to Rocker, Major League Baseball demanded he undergo a drug test at the time. And in a book published in 2011, Rocker revealed he was taking steroids and surely must have tested positive for the substance. "Let's be honest, who wasn't [using steroids]?" Rocker told the radio host Mike Silva. "I'm not going to step on that mound with that kind of responsibility with my gun half loaded." Still, nobody with Major League Baseball ever said or did anything about this test.

Rocker's first trip back to Shea Stadium after the infamous interview occurred in late June 2000 and was quite the circus. The New York tabloids had by then dubbed him "Johnny Rotten," and Mets fans were salivating for a chance at retribution. There was a peace offering: Rocker gave a videotaped apology on the big scoreboard screen. He did not, however, ride the 7 train to the stadium as he had promised. The team limited beer sales during the game, a protective cover was placed over the Braves' bullpen, and some seven hundred police officers were assigned to the ballpark. Rocker pitched one hitless, scoreless inning.

By 2001, when he was still only twenty-six years old, Rocker's fastball was losing steam, and he blew too many saves. Given his decreasing efficiency, the Braves had no reason to retain such a troublemaker and sent him packing to Cleveland, who later moved him to Texas. He briefly signed as a free agent with Tampa Bay in June 2003, but by then he couldn't throw faster than the mid-eighties. Those last years in the majors weren't pretty. In limited appearances, his ERA went from 4.32 in 2001, to 6.66 in 2002, to 9.00 in 2003. Rocker wouldn't give up the hunt and eventually became part of another crazy spectacle by signing in 2005 with the independent minor-league team the Long Island Ducks. There, he failed miserably again, with a 6.50 ERA in twenty-three games. Despite being protected in Central Islip by a public relations agent at all times and by a closed dugout, Rocker managed to make a fool of himself again by comparing his problems to those of black pioneers like Jackie Robinson and Hank Aaron.

"I've taken a lot of crap from a lot of people," Rocker told ESPN. "Probably more than anybody in the history of this sport. I know Hank and Jackie took a good deal of crap, but I guarantee it wasn't for six years. I just keep thinking: How much am I supposed to take? It's still there—the same force that it's always been. Most anybody else would have quit five years ago. I don't have to deal with the media scrutiny, the fan scrutiny, the mental persecution I get put through, the hatred and negative energy on a daily basis."

In Rocker's own twisted mind, he had endured far more suffering than the minorities he insulted.

STEVE HOWE AND HIS FATAL HABIT

Steve Howe had a golden arm and an addictive personality to ruin it. Baseball people kept giving him second, third, and fourth chances, and the talented lefty just kept letting teammates down with his performance-sabotaging drug problems. Altogether, Howe would be suspended seven times in his career, chronically lying to himself and others in order to get back into the sport. It got to the point where he became such a symbol for drug enabling that his name was dropped in a 1994 Hollywood comedy. "This is your last chance," Leslie Nielsen's character says in the film *Naked Gun 33⅓* to Anna Nicole Smith's character. "And I'm not talking about one of those Major League Baseball Steve Howe kind of last chances."

Howe began his career brilliantly enough. A Big Ten star at the University of Michigan, he was selected by the Dodgers in the first round of the 1979 amateur draft, cast as a reliever, and became the National League Rookie of the Year in 1980, at age twenty-two, with a rookie-record seventeen saves. In 1981, Howe closed out the deciding Game 6 of the World Series against the Yankees after taking the mound in the sixth inning. His blazing fastball became even more unhittable over the next two seasons, but Howe was already battling his addiction. He sought treatment for cocaine use for the first time after the 1982 season, then relapsed and entered a drug rehab center on May 29, 1983, missing more than a month. His cocaine use was not yet impairing Howe's pitching at this juncture, just his life. When he checked into the drug center, Howe had not yet yielded a single earned run in his first fourteen appearances of the season. His habit would affect his eligibility, however, if nothing else. On September 23, 1983, he was suspended after missing the Dodgers' flight to Atlanta and refusing a urinalysis. Howe had a 1.44 ERA at the time yet was ruled unavailable to Los Angeles during the Dodgers' National League Championship Series loss to the Phillies.

In December, Commissioner Bowie Kuhn suspended Howe for the entire 1984 season, a penalty that would cost the pitcher about $450,000. When Howe returned for 1985, he was no longer the same pitcher, and the Dodgers no longer wanted to deal with his chaos. He was released in July and picked up by the

Twins. In Minnesota, matters didn't improve. Toward the end of the season, he appeared on ABC's *Nightline*, talking about his cocaine problems and his difficulties dealing with simple day-to-day routines. "Life in general and people and places and things and success a lot of times are people's problems," Howe said. "At least it was for me."

While he spoke of his addiction in the past tense, that wasn't at all the case. One day after his appearance on the program, Howe went AWOL. Three days later, he showed up, requested his release from the Twins, and again checked into rehab. On it went like this, as ambitious general managers kept hoping to tame Howe's compulsions while unleashing his fastball. He was a flop for Texas in 1987 and took four years off while writing a book, *Between the Lines: One Athlete's Struggle to Escape the Nightmare of Addiction.* Improbably, Howe reemerged with considerable success for the Yankees in 1991. George Steinbrenner always enjoyed rehabilitating fallen stars such as Howe and Darryl Strawberry in the Bronx. Perhaps redemption for others meant redemption for Steinbrenner's own, very different sins. Howe was lights out in three of his first four seasons in pinstripes, with ERAs of 1.68, 2.45, and 1.80. He wasn't cured of his disease, however. On June 8, 1992, Howe was suspended from baseball for what was by then the seventh time after pleading guilty to a misdemeanor charge of attempting to buy cocaine. Sixteen days later, Commissioner Fay Vincent banned him permanently. That penalty was overturned by an arbitrator in November, and Howe signed again with the Yanks for the 1993 season without missing a beat.

Howe was still part of the Yanks in 1996, their championship season, until his release in June. He was dumped more for some bad performances than for his drug problems. Howe was clearly unraveling. Two days later, on June 24, he was arrested at Kennedy Airport for carrying a loaded gun in his luggage. This kind of story could only end badly, and so it did. On April 28,

2006, Howe was killed at age forty-eight when his pickup truck drifted into a median and then off a desert highway, rolling over in Coachella, California. A coroner's report indicated he had methamphetamines in his system at the time of the crash, an addict until the end.

"My sole existence of what I did in life was what I did on the ballfield," Howe had said. "When nothing else matters and you don't feel that you're going to be able to perform up to your capabilities and someone gives you an avenue to deaden that pain, you're going to do what you can do."

GUS WEYHING AND THE GREAT PIGEON THEFT OF 1892

By all accounts, Gus Weyhing was a remarkably durable pitcher during a fourteen-year career from 1887 to 1901 with nine baseball teams. "Rubber-Winged Gus" was a man of slight stature, weighing as little as 120 pounds. Yet during the 1892 season with the Phillies, he threw 469⅔ innings and amassed forty-six complete games. Weyhing also threw a no-hitter in 1888 for the Kansas City Cowboys and that same season almost single-handedly eliminated the Brooklyn Bridegrooms from the pennant race with three successive complete-game victories over that American Association team in the same week. By today's standards, these feats would earn Weyhing his own wing in the Hall of Fame.

Weyhing, however, had some very rough edges. For one thing, he was wild on the mound, infuriating teammates and opponents alike. He hit more batters, 277, than anyone else in history. In his first two seasons alone, he hit 79 batters to lead the league both years. It would be tempting to suggest Weyhing was mean on the mound, but the stats seem to indicate he simply had major control problems. He threw 105 wild pitches in those same two years and in 1889 walked 212 hitters. By comparison, the nastiest starters of the modern era could not come close to these numbers. Bob Gibson plunked only 102 batters in seventeen seasons, while Roger Clemens nailed 159 batters in twenty-four years—and nearly six hundred more innings pitched than Weyhing.

And then there were the pigeons, Weyhing's longtime hobby. Not long before the start of Weyhing's signature season, he was brought before the Louisville, Kentucky, police court on a charge of grand larceny. A local Louisville newspaper reported the incident this way on January 26, 1892:

> During the past two days a number of pigeons have been stolen from the coops at the National Pigeon Show, and last night, when Weyhing started out of the building with his basket, a pair of blondinettes, valued at $100, were found in his possession. He could not explain how he got the birds, and was therefore arrested. The case was continued and he was released on bail. Weyhing has a weakness for fine pigeons; in fact, is quite a pigeon fancier, and this fact makes the charge appear plausible. It does not, however, seem possible that a man in Weyhing's position, and with such an income as he enjoys, would be guilty of such a deed for a couple of birds. Weyhing has in the past been in trouble through indiscretion, but nothing more serious than conviviality, and consequent excesses, was ever charged against him. It is to be hoped, however, for his own sake, as well as for the sake of the Philadelphia Club and the good repute of the profession, that the charge against him is unfounded. If he should not be able to clear himself it would be a hard blow to the Philadelphia Club, which had counted on Weyhing as its star pitcher next season.

From here, things get blurry. Charges may have been dropped or fines paid. We know at least that Weyhing was not seriously disciplined. He started the season on schedule with the Phillies, earning his ample $3,250 salary with a career year. There are no stats available on the pigeons.

DAVE KINGMAN AND HIS WAR ON THE FOURTH ESTATE

If you ever had the pleasure of talking to the longtime Mets public relations man Jay Horwitz, he would swear to you that Dave Kingman was a cooperative fellow in the clubhouse. This was very hard to believe for those reporters who were forced to cover Kingman during many of his sixteen seasons in the majors. There was an ugly, undeclared war waged for much of that time between this player and the media.

Reporters generally divide baseball players into three categories when it comes to working relationships: players who actually enjoy conversing with writers; players who comply with interview requests mainly because they understand it is part of their job (this category probably represents the majority); and players who resent the intrusion and refuse to deal with the media at all. Kingman fell into a fourth category. He initiated conflict. There was no obvious reason for this, other than perhaps some bitterness on Kingman's part that he wasn't receiving ample credit for his power numbers. He was no isolated bumpkin, so that was no excuse. Kingman played a couple of years at the University of Southern California before turning pro. But he just kept getting nastier with reporters. If he struck a game-winning homer, he would typically go out of his way to tell writers on tight deadlines to wait at his locker, promising to speak to them about his feat after he showered. Thirty minutes later, Kingman would walk, smirking, past the same group of reporters and head to his car without a word, carrying a six-pack of beer.

This sort of antisocial behavior might have been forgiven, but then Kingman crossed several lines during his final year of baseball in 1986. The reporter Sue Fornoff of *The Sacramento Bee* was sitting in the press box during the first inning of a game when a pink box was delivered to her from Kingman. Inside was a live rat with a note tied to its tail. "My name is Sue," the note said. After the game, Kingman didn't deny this was his doing. "This is a man's clubhouse," he said. "If someone can't take a simple joke, they shouldn't be in the game." Kingman had been particularly antagonistic toward women writers during his career. The Oakland A's fined him $3,500 for this stunt, and he was warned that another such deed would mean the end of his career.

Writers had the last laugh on Kingman, when they made him the first 400-homer player not to be elected into the Hall of Fame. That was no surprise, considering Kingman's career batting average was .236, he had struck out 1,816 times, and he was considered a lousy outfielder and first baseman. What was shocking, though, was that Kingman received only three votes from writers in his first year of eligibility in 1992, meaning a player with 442 lifetime homers had been immediately eliminated on his first ballot.

As a batter, Kingman was a tremendous all-or-nothing spectacle. He could drive a ball 530 feet and blasted three homers in a game five times during his career. Kingman was far more likely to strike out, however, and with his low on-base percentage became the ultimate anti-Moneyball player in pre–Billy Beane Oakland. With the Mets in 1982, Kingman led the league in homers (thirty-seven) and strikeouts (156) while batting only .204. He became famous that season for posting the lowest batting average ever by a home run leader and by a regular first baseman. Even odder: Kingman's batting average was lower than that of the Cy Young winner Steve Carlton, who hit .218. Carlton hated speaking to the press, too. But he never sent a rat to the press box.

KEN CAMINITI AND THE VERY PUBLIC CONFESSION

Ken Caminiti never met a drug he didn't like—or, at least, a drug he couldn't resist. Some of his self-medication was performance enhancing; some was performance diminishing. Almost none of it was legal, however, and greatly contributed to a premature death in 2004 at age forty-one. Along the way, he also became one of baseball's pioneer whistle-blowers on the steroid front, viewed as something of a rat fink by teammates.

Fatally flawed as he was, there was never much wrong with Caminiti at the plate or around third base. He thrived for most of his fifteen seasons in the majors, though his career arc was extremely suspicious. After eight years in which he never hit more than eighteen homers during a single season, Caminiti exploded in his early thirties into a holy terror at bat. During a particularly golden four-season stretch for the Padres, from 1995 to 1998, Caminiti was a two-time All-Star, a three-time Gold Glove winner, and the National League Most Valuable Player in 1996 while batting .326 with forty homers and 130 RBIs. He also was very much juiced at the time, which he later confirmed. In June 2002, Caminiti broke through the cone of silence regarding steroid use in baseball, practically bragging in an interview with *Sports Illustrated* about the proliferation of drugs.

"It's no secret what's going on in baseball," Caminiti said.

At least half the guys are using steroids. They talk about it. They joke about it with each other. The guys who want to protect themselves or their image by lying have that right. Me? I'm at the point in my career where I've done just about every bad thing you can do. I try to walk with my head up. I don't have to hold my tongue. I don't want to hurt teammates or friends. But I've got nothing to hide. If a young player were to ask me what to do, I'm not going to tell him it's bad. Look at all the money in the game. You have a chance to set your family up, to get your daughter into a better school. . . . So I can't say, "Don't do it," not when the guy next to you is as big as a house and he's going to take your job and make the money.

There was considerable skepticism at the time about Caminiti's public contentions, particularly his statement that half the players in baseball were juiced. But Caminiti had no reason to lie, little to gain or lose by then. He'd been released by his last team, Atlanta, and earned more than $37 million in his career. Later testing would reveal that he might have exaggerated the numbers a bit, but steroid use was endemic in many clubhouses during the 1990s and early years of the twenty-first century. Caminiti wasn't just ingesting drugs that improved his power numbers, however. He also struggled throughout his short life with alcohol and cocaine. As early as 1994, he spoke of battling alcohol and painkiller addictions and later checked himself into rehab. He was arrested in 2001 for possession of cocaine, then court ordered into a treatment center in 2003 when he tested positive for cocaine while on probation. In September 2004, Caminiti tested positive yet again for cocaine, the fourth failed drug test since he had been placed on probation. He was released by the court for time served—which turned out to be a terrible mistake. Within a week of that court appearance, Caminiti died in the Bronx on October 10, 2004, of what was ruled "acute intoxication due to the combined effects of cocaine and opiates" that had weakened his heart. "There's nothing in the report that changes the enormous amount of love that Ken had in his heart for his family, his friends, and his teammates," said Rick Licht, Caminiti's agent and lawyer.

ERIC SHOW, ANTIHERO

Eric Show was a smart, guitar-playing kid with an overbearing father and a great talent for throwing a baseball. Drafted in the eighteenth round by the Padres in 1978 out of the University of California, Riverside, Show had plenty of opinions—some quirky, some downright offensive—and fought at length with his first big-league manager, Dick Williams. Show would criticize Williams for taking him out of a game early, and then the next time Williams would just leave Show on the mound to take an incessant pounding. Show was considered an oddball by his more conventional teammates. "We would talk about baseball," Goose Gossage told ESPN. "And he would start to get real heavy. I'd say, 'Wait a minute, Eric, we're better off keeping it as simple as it is.' But there was no reasoning with Eric. . . . Pretty soon, I didn't even talk to him."

By then, Show had his own set of friends in the clubhouse, his fellow Padres pitchers Dave Dravecky and Mark Thurmond. Teammates nicknamed the trio the Pep Boys, and the group was quite the handful. Show was the philosophical leader, determining policy while still searching for cosmic answers. The Pep Boys decided women reporters weren't welcome in the clubhouse. Soon, after walking into a bookstore filled with ultra-right-wing material, Show informed everyone he had become a member of the John Birch Society. "Ronald Reagan is too far left for me," he declared. "I'd realized there was a problem in the world, and I'd deduced conspiracy."

The three Pep Boys went to a local fair in 1984 to hand out John Birch literature—viewed as anti-Semitic and racist in many quarters. Show campaigned against Social Security, the graduated income tax, and the United Nations. At the same time, he would demonstrate a more progressive, charitable side. He would hand out money to strangers, sponsor a black missionary, and shake his head at his own bloated salary—which grew to $1.45 million in 1989, when age and injuries began to catch up with him.

Back in 1984, the Padres were heading to the World Series, and Show was on his way to winning fifteen games for the second straight season. San Diego was a conservative place. Fans were willing to forgive Show's political leanings and his seemingly arrogant musings. "As long as air has weight, I'll have a slider," Show said. Still, lousy performances in the 1984 playoffs left him branded with the reputation as a choker. Then, on September 11, 1985, Show hung a slider and gave up the record-breaking 4,192nd hit to Pete Rose, which was believed at the time to have surpassed Ty Cobb's record (historians later adjusted Cobb's hit total downward by two). Show was less than gracious about the event. He sat on the mound appearing uninterested while Rose's feat was celebrated all around him. "In the eternal scheme of things," Show said, "how much does this matter? I don't like to say this, but I don't care."

Things went downhill for Show after that. Dravecky and Thurmond, his best pals, were both traded. During a game in July 1987, Show nailed the Cubs' star Andre Dawson with a fastball to the head after Dawson homered off him in the first inning. Dawson went after Show, and there was a bench-clearing brawl that clearly shook up the pitcher. Show ended up penning a handwritten letter of apology to Dawson.

Show's career found a second wind in 1988—sixteen wins with a 3.26 ERA—but at a steep price. He had begun to use amphetamines in a big way, and by the next season he was on crystal meth, later cocaine. He was an addict, unreliable and no longer worth the trouble. He signed briefly in Oakland for the 1991 season, until he got in a scrape with police and Tony La Russa released him. "If the stuff doesn't change, what's the use of having him?" La Russa said. Show was hallucinating and suffering from paranoid delusions. Finally, sadly, he checked himself out of a drug rehab center against doctors' recommendations and went on a terrible drug binge. According to reports, Show ingested four $10 bags of cocaine and eight $10 bags of heroin and then downed a six-pack of beer. He died on the morning of March 16, 1994, of an apparent heart attack at the age of thirty-seven, forever uncomfortable in his own skin.

MIKE KEKICH AND FRITZ PETERSON, SWINGMEN

Mike Kekich was a left-handed starter for five different teams over nine seasons in the major leagues. He did not perform this job particularly well, finishing with a 4.59 ERA during a span from the mid-1960s through the early 1970s when the average ERA was typically under 4.00. But it was the 1973 season that immortalized Kekich forever as part of one of the quirkiest feel-bad stories in baseball lore. It was so weird, in fact, that Ben Affleck bought the movie rights for a project he envisioned with his pal Matt Damon.

Before the season began, Kekich and his fellow Yankees starter Fritz Peterson traded wives and families the way the Yankees often traded players. Kekich hooked up with Marilyn Peterson, while Peterson paired off with Susanne Kekich. Even in this period of sexual liberation—the movie *Bob & Carol & Ted & Alice* had premiered four years earlier—such an arrangement was shocking by all baseball club standards. Two mop-haired hipsters had invaded the most sanctified of clubhouses in the Bronx. The swap between the families actually was first discussed among them in 1972, during an outdoor summer party at the house of the late sportswriter Maury Allen, who overheard conversations about the plan. "We had a tremendous amount of affection and compatibility all around," Kekich would tell the New York *Daily News*. "By American standards, I had a good marriage. But I wanted a great marriage. I was idealistic, I guess. I can't tell you how perfect it would have been if it had worked."

The pitchers made the switch in October, though the Yankees didn't announce the transaction until spring training of 1973. "We didn't trade wives," Kekich said. "We traded lives." The incident was a terrible embarrassment to the once-staid Yankees, who were already roiling in rapid transition after the team was sold to a group headed by George Steinbrenner. Faced with a public relations disaster, the club executive Lee MacPhail quipped, "We may have to call off Family Day this season." The club suddenly had a new owner, a designated hitter, and a pair of swingers in its starting rotation. Jake Gibbs, a catcher for the Yankees through 1971, told the *Clarion-Ledger* in Jackson, Mississippi, "Fritz and Mike were good friends. They were

Mike Kekich and Fritz Peterson swapped families in very un-Yankee-like fashion.
AP Photo/Marty Lederhandler

really close, and their families were close. I guess we just didn't know how close. . . . Of course, they were both left-handers. You can never tell about lefties."

Of the two lefties, there was no doubt Kekich was the less effective pitcher. He'd originally been signed as a prospect to a $50,000 bonus by the Dodgers for his impressive fastball, but that pitch was utterly uncontrollable. "Fritz had great stuff and super control," Gibbs said. "He had some great years. Kekich had good stuff, but he didn't always know where it was going." Kekich was horrid on the mound in 1973, with a 7.52 ERA in twenty-one appearances for both the Yankees and the Indians. The Yanks dumped him on Cleveland in a deal for Lowell Palmer in June. Palmer, a notable disaster in his own right with a 5.29 career ERA, never threw a pitch for the Yanks, who were just happy to be rid of the whole Peterson-Kekich drama. Palmer was fast and notoriously wild (he issued 202 walks and flung thirty-five wild pitches in 316⅔ innings), but only while pitching. That was an improvement from Kekich.

The family swap had two very different endings. Peterson's performance also declined, but he married Susanne, and the newly formed couple produced four children of their own. Peterson worked at odd jobs, found religion, and wrote a book in 2009, *Mickey Mantle Is Going to Heaven*. He rather self-righteously predicted to *New York* magazine that Kekich would likely spend some time in hell. Meanwhile, Mike Kekich and Marilyn Peterson never worked out. Besides stints pitching in Cleveland, Texas, and Seattle, Kekich played for clubs in Japan and Mexico. Eventually, he remarried, moved to Albuquerque, and became an insurance adjuster. But 1973 will forever be remembered as the season Kekich swapped wives, posted a 7.52 ERA, and was dealt to Cleveland for a pitcher everyone knew was terrible. "Neither Fritz Peterson nor I will ever make it into the Hall of Fame," Kekich once said. Clearly, there is another path to fame, the road less traveled.

JEFF KENT, BATTING BEHIND BARRY BONDS

Jeff Kent was a five-time All-Star, a National League MVP, and the all-time home run leader among second basemen. He also was a resentful loner, winning the animosity of teammates along with all his other awards. His reputation as an isolationist was first forged with the Mets during his rookie season in

1992, when Kent refused to participate in the silly, harmless hazing ritual that required rookies to dress in drag for a few hours. Kent said he'd been there, done that already in Toronto, where he'd played before a mid-season trade. On the other hand, to his credit, Kent willingly agreed to play shortstop for one game that year so that Willie Randolph could start at second base in his final game.

So far, not so bad. But Kent was traded to Cleveland, then to San Francisco, where he and Barry Bonds eventually became the most talented, unpleasant one-two tandem in baseball. Bonds had his personal trainer, his personal chair, his personal transportation on the road. Kent had the feeling he was overshadowed and underappreciated. The two stars clashed and confronted each other on several occasions, which became a sticky problem for the manager, Dusty Baker.

When Kent first arrived, he actually was quite popular with the Giants. His teammates voted for him to receive the Willie Mac Award in 1998, an honor named after Willie McCovey representing good leadership and spirit. He won the league MVP award in 2000, beating out Bonds, but soon frittered away everyone's admiration and good faith. Kent fractured his wrist during spring training in 2002, claiming it happened while he was washing his truck. It was later revealed he had suffered the injury while performing fanciful stunts on his motorcycle, in violation of his contract. In June 2002, Kent and the third baseman David Bell got into a screaming argument after they botched a force-out at second base against the Padres. Bonds came over in the dugout to stick up for Bell, and there, for cameras and notepads to record, the feud came to a public boil. Kent and Bonds screamed and shoved each other before Baker pulled away Kent. "Add this to the half-dozen times we've done this before," said Kent, who insisted it was no big deal. "We had an emotional day both on the field and off."

Eventually, Kent was dealt to Houston and then to Los

Angeles, where he made few new friends. Interestingly, he has attended a few of the Hall of Fame induction ceremonies lately, which of course has led cynics to believe he is campaigning for his own election. Asked by *Baseball Digest* to describe his baseball credo, Kent answered, "Dedicated. I think I play the game with respect. . . . I'm old school and I play the game that way. I love to play the game. Everything else, I don't care much about." Everything else, unfortunately, included his teammates.

BOTTOM TEN

1	**JIMMY PIERSALL**	One of the great defensive outfielders before he made a career out of his own psychological problems.
2	**RUBÉN RIVERA**	Gave new meaning to the term "glove man."
3	**JOHN ROCKER**	Put a sock in it.
4	**STEVE HOWE**	Let everyone down in the end, including himself.
5	**GUS WEYHING**	Long before Mike Tyson, this man put pigeons on the map.
6	**DAVE KINGMAN**	Sexist rat sent sexist rat to woman reporter.
7	**KEN CAMINITI**	He broke the code of silence— only not at all like Jim Bouton.
8	**ERIC SHOW**	Right-hander went far right-wing.
9	**MIKE KEKICH and FRITZ PETERSON**	Swinging strike, at least for one of them.
10	**(tie) JEFF KENT DICK ALLEN MANNY RAMIREZ REGGIE JACKSON JIM BOUTON**	(Kent) The enemy of his teammates' enemy (Bonds) was not necessarily a friend. (Allen) He was suspended in 1969 for visiting a racehorse instead of showing up for a Phillies doubleheader. (Ramirez) "Manny being Manny" was only sometimes fun. Always knew when it was his contract year. (Jackson) The straw that stirred the drink infuriated Thurman Munson and Billy Martin. (Bouton) First one to tell all, and break with tradition.

10 EVEN STEROIDS DIDN'T HELP
The Most Pathetic Juiceheads of All Time

PLAYERS LIKE BARRY Bonds, Mark McGwire, and Manny Ramirez fortified their bodies and lengthened their careers with the use of performance-enhancing drugs. But for every successful cheater, there have been many players who tried the stuff and still stank up the joint.

By 2012, sixty-six major-league players and former major-league players had been suspended because they tested positive for performance-enhancing drugs. The majority of these offenders were little known and had fairly lousy careers. The drugs cost these guys their reputations without improving their batting averages, their ERAs, or their bank accounts.

DUSTIN RICHARDSON, RECORD BREAKER

Dustin Richardson was a little-known pitcher with the Red Sox in 2009 and 2010, but he soon smashed every major-league mark known to man. In January 2012, Major League Baseball confirmed that Richardson had tested positive the previous November for no fewer than five prohibited substances—three of those drugs being the anabolic steroids trenbolone, methandienone, and methenolone. On top of that, his urine sample showed evidence of letrozole, a drug that can disguise the by-products of steroid use, plus a more conventional amphetamine. This was a precedent-setting number, not only in baseball, but in all amateur and professional sports governed by drug testing. Stacking drugs to increase efficacy or to mask the use of other drugs is not uncommon, but nobody could remember the stack rising quite so high.

Dustin Richardson stretching his muscles, which were chemically enhanced by five different substances prohibited by Major League Baseball.
AP Photo/Nati Harnik

At the time these tests were confirmed, Richardson had just been released by the Atlanta Braves. And while the left-hander would not comment on the findings, his mother insisted her son was regretful. "Dustin realizes it was the biggest mistake of his life," Debra Richardson told *The New York Times.* "He was so ashamed. I'm praying someone will give him another chance." Dustin Richardson was twenty-eight years old at the time of this disclosure, when he was ordered to serve a fifty-game suspension if he ever returned to the majors. He had been drafted by the Tigers in the thirty-ninth round of the 2003 amateur draft, decided to pitch for Texas Tech instead, and was eventually selected by Boston in the fifth round of the 2006 draft. He became a minor celebrity of sorts by appearing on the ESPN reality show *Knight School,* as one of the finalists for a walk-on spot on Bobby Knight's basketball team.

The lanky, six-foot, six-inch pitcher had thrown only sixteen and one-third innings with the Red Sox in relief, walking fifteen batters while posting a 3.31 ERA, before he was traded to the Florida Marlins and assigned to the minors. "It's a clubhouse full of veterans," Richardson said about the atmosphere at Fenway. "There's a lot more pressure to do well, especially with the fans, and just in Boston, the pressure to win in general. I think I put too much pressure on myself. I learned a lot of the way you go about the game, respect for the game."

Those words never rang more hollow than when Richardson was nailed for multidrug abuse. In a way, you could almost understand his desperation. He had not fared well in Triple-A games during 2011, combining for a 4.79 ERA with New Orleans of the Pacific Coast League and Gwinnett of the International League. Whatever drugs he was taking at the time did not aid his control problems, because Richardson walked forty-two minor leaguers in sixty-two innings. When the Marlins had acquired Richardson in 2010, the club's president, Larry Beinfest, said Richardson had considerable potential, if only he could gain control of his pitches. "He has good minor-league numbers," Beinfest said. "We think there's upside with this kid." Beinfest had no idea what sort of up was in the upside.

ALEX SÁNCHEZ, THE WRONG KIND OF PIONEER

The first player in major-league history to be suspended after testing positive for performance-enhancing drugs hit a grand total of six homers in 1,527 at-bats, which would seem to indicate something was amiss. The numbers never made much sense, which was Alex Sánchez's primary defense in April 2005. Why would a leadoff hitter, a base stealer, try to beef up on an undisclosed muscle builder? Apparently, though, Sánchez did just that. The only question was whether he did so intentionally or consumed an illegal supplement accidentally.

"I know I did nothing incorrect," Sánchez said at the time. "I take stuff I buy over the counter . . . something to give me energy, put a little muscle on my body. That's it. Multivitamins, protein shakes, muscle relaxants. That kind of stuff. Look at what kind of player I am. I'm a leadoff hitter. I never hit any home runs."

He was right about that part, but it didn't stop baseball from enforcing its new drug policy and suspending Sánchez for ten games at the very beginning of the 2005 season. This was a new world. Each player was now responsible for everything he swallowed and put in his body, same as an Olympic athlete. Sánchez didn't bother to appeal the suspension. Lou Piniella, Tampa Bay's manager, had planned to start Sánchez, twenty-eight, in center field and use him as his leadoff guy. He had batted .322 with nineteen stolen bases in seventy-nine games in 2004 for the Tigers, who had released him nonetheless due to his chronic leg problems and defensive liabilities. The Rays picked up Sánchez for a mere $316,000, figuring they had nothing to lose. As it turned out, they did. The team nurtured a family-oriented image, and this suspension became a great embarrassment. Sánchez was essentially dropped by Tampa Bay on June 13, 2005, even though he was batting .346. Piniella couldn't abide his fielding problems, and ownership didn't want to deal with the drug stigma. He signed with the Giants but was quickly injured and then released again.

That was it for Sánchez, who had come such a long way at tremendous personal sacrifice just to throw away his career like this. In 1994, at the age of eighteen, Sánchez had risked life and limb by clambering aboard a homemade raft and sailing from Cuba toward Florida, leaving his family behind. He was stopped by the Coast Guard after three days and detained for sixteen months at Guantánamo before finally reaching Miami. There, he attended community college and was drafted in the fifth round by Tampa Bay in the 1996 entry draft. Sánchez eventually became a U.S. citizen in 2004 and then was reunited in Miami with his mother and brother in 2005, just one month before he was busted by the urinalysis. Sánchez's timing was never great. In the end, he finished with total career earnings of about $1.2 million—

a good deal of money for a Cuban refugee, yet so much less than he might have amassed if not for a single positive test.

RYAN FRANKLIN, MARINER NIGHTMARE

Ryan Franklin was an utter disaster for the Seattle Mariners, from both a performance and a public relations standpoint. This was all the more shocking considering his backstory as one of the all-American heroes of the U.S. Olympic gold-medal baseball zteam at Sydney in 2000, when the pitcher went 3-0 in four appearances.

Franklin was busted on a positive test in May 2005, suspended in August for ten days, then went on to complete a season with an ERA of 5.10 in which he gave up twenty-eight homers in thirty starts. In fact, from 2003 through 2005, Franklin yielded ninety-five homers in ninety-six appearances. Over his final three seasons in Seattle as a starter, he was 23-44. Arguably worse than those stats, however, he brought shame upon the Mariners organization, not only with the steroid use, but with his stubborn denials in the face of overwhelming proof.

After the test and punishment were made public, Franklin went on the offensive. "There has to be a flaw in the system, I have no clue," he said. "There is a flaw in the testing or my urine got mixed up with somebody else's. They said that couldn't happen, but I don't believe it. I just know deep in my heart that I'd never do anything like that." Then, in the 2007 *Mitchell Report*, Franklin was named as one of a dozen former Mariners who procured performance-enhancing drugs. Investigators found Franklin had been referred to the steroid salesman Kirk Radomski by his Seattle teammate the pitcher Ron Villone. "Villone called Radomski and told him to send Anavar and Deca-Durabolin [two anabolic steroids] to Franklin, and Radomski did so," the report concluded.

Franklin never confessed to anything, bouncing around the National League as a middle reliever, then reinventing himself as a closer with the Cardinals. He had one inexplicable All-Star season in 2009, when he earned thirty-eight saves with a 1.92 ERA. Then it was back to mediocrity, or worse. During the first three weeks of the 2011 season, Franklin was last in the majors, he blew a save on Opening Day, blew another save, and lost two games. He was soon demoted to setup man, somehow managing to hang in there for twenty-one games, collecting his $3.25 million salary from the Cardinals despite a 1-4 mark and an ERA of 8.46. Finally, he was released in mid-season and hired on as a scout for the remainder of his pact. He returned to his ranch in Spiro, Oklahoma, with his wife and three kids. "It was pretty neat to be able to take my kids on their first day of school," Franklin said. Hopefully, his children will not be studying the history of the Seattle Mariners.

EDINSON VÓLQUEZ, A DISAPPOINTMENT BY ANY NAME

If Edinson Vólquez did nothing but get traded from the Rangers to the Reds for Josh Hamilton, he'd already be an infamous disaster in Cincinnati. Instead, he added to his legacy there with a drug suspension, an elbow problem, and a steep decline into the statistical netherworld. While Hamilton was batting .359, with thirty-two homers and a hundred RBIs in Texas during his 2010 MVP season, Vólquez appeared in only twelve games, winning four of them with a 4.31 ERA.

But that was only part of the story with Vólquez, who went by so many names it is hard to pin his disappointing career on any one of them. He was signed in 2001 as a top prospect at age seventeen out of the Dominican Republic, going at the time by the name Julio Reyes. In 2003, concerned about immigration inquiries, he became Edison Vólquez, considerably closer to his birth name. In 2007, he informed the Texas Rangers and the Topps company that his first name was Edinson on his birth certificate. He had by then appeared on baseball cards with three different names. To make matters even more confusing, he preferred the nickname Pedrito, or "Little Pedro," because he idolized Pedro Martínez.

When Vólquez was called up to Texas in August 2005 after four years in the minors, he was horrid. He went 0-4 with a 14.21 ERA in six games. Then, in 2006, he was 1-6 with a 7.29 ERA. His problems went beyond the record. The Rangers were concerned that Vólquez appeared indifferent. He wasn't watching the games from the bench, didn't bother to tuck his jersey into his pants, and didn't follow a regular workout routine. Texas officials demoted Vólquez all the way down to Class A ball, gave him a laundry list of to-dos, and hoped he could harness his fastball, tame his control problems, and become a more diligent professional. Vólquez did well enough to regain his status as a top, tradable prospect. On December 21, 2007, the Rangers were able to send him to Cincinnati along with the erratic pitcher Danny Herrera for Hamilton.

Even when it all came together in 2008 for Vólquez during an All-Star season in Cincinnati—he was 17-6 with a 3.21 ERA and 206 strikeouts—the pitcher led the league in hit batsmen with fourteen. Vólquez fared so well that year the Reds began crowing about how they had made a steal in the deal for Hamilton. "I don't know if I can say it, but I'm going to say it: the Texas Rangers made a mistake in trading him away," Francisco Cordero, the Reds' closer, told ESPN.com.

By the next spring, however, Vólquez's ephemeral competence had vanished. There were hints of that already at the World Baseball Classic in March 2009, as Vólquez became the losing pitcher in the opening game for the Dominican Republic, giving up three runs to the Netherlands in three innings. Then, during the regular season, he was 4-2, with a 4.35 ERA, when he was placed on the sixty-day disabled list with an elbow injury and headed off for Tommy John surgery. Nothing went right after that. Perhaps by accident, perhaps out of desperation, Vólquez ingested a performance-enhancing drug in 2010. Still only twenty-six years old, still on the disabled list, he failed the urine test in spring training and was suspended for fifty games. The pitcher claimed it was all a terrible misunderstanding and that the positive test was caused by a prescription drug from his native Dominican Republic he was taking in order to facilitate reproduction with his wife. This was an innovative alibi, if nothing else.

"I understand that I must accept responsibility for this mistake and have chosen not to challenge my suspension," Vólquez said. "I want to assure everyone that this was an isolated incident involving my genuine effort to treat a common medical issue. I was not trying in any way to gain an advantage in my baseball career."

He was sent back down to Class A, then made a modest comeback in 2010 before falling apart again in 2011 with a 5-7 mark and a 5.71 ERA in twenty starts. Finally, Vólquez and the Reds parted ways as he and his $2.237 million contract were dumped on San Diego in a multiplayer deal for the young pitcher Mat Latos. Vólquez enjoyed some success with the Padres heading into his arbitration year, and there wasn't a general manager on the planet who could predict this pitcher's future.

FÉLIX HEREDIA, HANGING ON

Pitchers don't always use performance-enhancing drugs with an eye on the Cy Young trophy. Sometimes, they just want to heal from injury, forge an unlikely comeback, and grab one last contract. Félix Heredia was apparently one such marginal case, already falling apart at the seams when he was suspended in

October 2005, becoming the eleventh major-league player to be disciplined for the use of a steroid.

Heredia was a journeyman middle reliever with control problems for seven years who suddenly enjoyed one effective season in 2003 during his contract year with the Reds and the Yankees—raising eyebrows in some quarters. He briefly became a crucial role player for the Yanks as a lefty coming out of the bullpen to face one or two lefty batters. He appeared in five of the seven games in the 2003 American League Championship Series against the Red Sox, throwing two and two-thirds hitless innings during that epic New York victory. Heredia then completely fell apart the next season, posting a disastrous 6.28 ERA with the Yanks in forty-seven appearances and becoming the object of great derision in New York. When he entered a game against the Twins during the American League Division Series, Heredia immediately plunked Corey Koskie in the back and hit Lew Ford in the ankle, giving up two runs and pitching his way out of Joe Torre's future plans. "I was trying to throw too hard and the ball was running in too much" was Heredia's explanation that day. The Yanks had seen and heard enough. After the 2004 season—and a seven-game series against the Red Sox that the Yankees will forever want to forget—the Bombers dumped Heredia on their poor sisters, the Mets, who picked up the $1.8 million price tag in the hopes that Heredia would become their setup man. Instead, he became one of Omar Minaya's worst fiascoes, almost from day one. In spring training, he sat out two weeks with a numb hand, then returned for a one-inning exhibition outing against the Yankees, walking the first two hitters he faced, then making an error on the next play. The Mets' manager, Willie Randolph, termed Heredia "a work in progress," but he never progressed.

The lefty made a grand total of three appearances and two and two-thirds innings during the regular season before he went on the disabled list in April with a strained left thumb and an aneurysm in his left shoulder. Heredia never pitched in the big leagues again after the ten-game suspension was handed down in October. Representatives for Heredia argued the positive test might have been the result of a tainted supplement or could have been caused by blood thinners used in medication during surgery. "We're trying to figure out exactly what it is," his agent, Martin Arburua, said about the positive test. "Whatever it was, though, he did not knowingly take it. He wasn't playing and had no reason to. He was trying to rehab and get back."

That of course may have been reason enough. Many athletes have turned to steroids and human growth hormone as one method of gaining strength following injury. As it turned out, the suspension hardly mattered. Heredia was done in the big leagues. He was signed to minor-league contracts by Arizona and Cleveland, assigned to a series of farm clubs where he posted ERAs of 6.75, 4.88, and 5.14 over the next three years. Heredia had earned more than $8.5 million during his ten-year career, plentiful compensation for twenty-eight victories, six saves, a 4.42 ERA, and a positive drug test.

BOTTOM TEN

1   **DUSTIN RICHARDSON**   Five strikes, you're out.

2   **ALEX SÁNCHEZ**   Pioneer juicer gets credit for being first one suspended.

3   **RYAN FRANKLIN**   From All-American to all-embarrassing.

4   **MANNY RAMIREZ**   Got old, then became first to break the three-digit barrier with 100-day suspension.

5   **EDINSON VÓLQUEZ**   Needs to change his name again.

6   **WILSON DELGADO**   Infielder played nine years in the majors, then was suspended twice for PEDs during his 2005 season in the minors.

7   **FÉLIX HEREDIA**   Nobody pitches for-ever, even on drugs.

8   **J. C. ROMERO**   Sued supplement makers and retailers to make up for $1.25 million in lost wages.

9   **JORGE TOCA**   Definition of desperate: four years after his last game in 2001 with the Mets, and in the majors, he was suspended fifteen days in the minors.

10   **MATT LAWTON**   Tested positive after batting .125 with the Yankees in 2005; had the good graces to apologize.

11 | THE SHOE-SHINE PITCH
The Luckiest Players of All Time

EVEN A STOPPED clock is right twice a day, and even a .200 hitter can bloop a single at the most serendipitous moment. Simply by statistical standard deviation, some very bad players are going to come up big at historically important moments and steal the spotlight from more meritorious teammates. Sometimes it seems that this "Mighty Mouse" phenomenon occurs more than expected in the major leagues, particularly around October. And when it does, yet another chronically underperforming player rewrites his entire career narrative with an indelible, happy plot twist. It is then left to baseball pundits to decide whether the fellow deserves plaudits for his heroic moment or condemnation for failing to live up to expectations the remainder of his career. Here, some very lucky athletes—plus one helpful spectator.

BRIAN DOYLE, SUPER GNAT

Brian Doyle was a slight, 160-pound utility infielder who barely batted his weight (.161) in 199 at-bats over four major-league seasons, from 1978 to 1981. He was the younger brother of Denny

Doyle, another second baseman with a somewhat more distinguished career. Brian would be less than a footnote in baseball
history, and certainly Yankees history, if not for the 1978 World
Series against the Los Angeles Dodgers.

Originally, Doyle was little more than a second-thought,
minor-league pickup by the Yanks in a deal that sent the aging
Sandy Alomar and his salary to the Texas Rangers before the
1977 season. When he was called up to the Bronx at the end of
April 1978, Doyle was shocked that he warranted a phone call
from George Steinbrenner, who had somehow taken an interest.
"Doyle, this is Steinbrenner," the phone call went. "I want you to
go out there and bust your butt and you better not disappoint
me." Then the Yankees' owner hung up the phone in typically
dramatic fashion.

Doyle's career narrative changed forever in October 1978,
largely because Willie Randolph's injured hamstring left a gap-
ing hole in the infield. Already, Randolph's absence had indirectly created one unlikely batting hero. In that famous playoff
game at Fenway against the Red Sox, Bucky Dent would likely
have been pulled for a pinch hitter if Randolph had been around
and the Yanks owned enough quality infielders on their depth
chart. Instead, Dent swung away and looped the game-winning
homer. That got the Yankees into the playoffs. Then Doyle batted .286 against the Royals in the American League Championship Series and became a potent gnat against the Dodgers in the
World Series, going 7 for 16 and batting .436 with a .500 slugging
percentage during the six-game Yankee victory.

In Game 1, a loss, Doyle was merely a late-innings replacement for Fred Stanley. He started Game 2, another loss, but it
really wasn't until Game 5, with the Series tied, that Doyle made
his mark by going 3 for 5 in that 12–2 victory at Yankee Stadium.
In Game 6, the clincher, Doyle was 3 for 4 in a 7–2 win. His double to deep left field in the second inning tied the score, 1–1. His

single to center on a 3-1 count in the sixth scored Lou Piniella for a 4–2 lead.

Doyle had moved up in weight class, met the moment head-on. By 1981, his last season, he was back to batting .125 for the Oakland A's.

"I wasn't a good player," Doyle said years later to *The Palm Beach Post*. "All you got to do is look at my bubble-gum card. It was definitely not because of my ability. It was being blessed at the right place, at the right time and having the mental capacity to block everything out and be focused."

Needless to say, Steinbrenner was thrilled with his second straight championship as an owner and with the little fellow who helped him get it. Steinbrenner told Doyle, "I knew you could do the job, that's why I went out and got you." To the owner's credit, Steinbrenner maintained contact with Doyle when the former player became very sick some sixteen years later. Doyle was diagnosed with leukemia and told he likely had only six months to live. "[Steinbrenner] said, 'You're a winner and you've always been a winner and you can beat this,'" Doyle told the New York *Daily News* of Steinbrenner's pep talks. "Just like that. He called constantly, every week, just to check up on me." Doyle underwent what was then a radical nine-month double-chemotherapy treatment that proved successful, and the disease went into remission. When he showed up for the 1995 Old-Timers' Day game at Yankee Stadium, he was invited into Steinbrenner's private box.

"I walked in and he said, 'I told you you were a winner,'" Doyle said. "Then we hugged and there were some tears. The affection I have for Mr. Steinbrenner is far and above the pinstripes."

PHIL LINZ AND HIS HARMONICA

Phil Linz was an unsung, but not unmusical, hero at the close of the Yankees' pennant run in the early 1960s. As a player of baseball, he wasn't much. The utility infielder had a .246 batting average in four years with the Yanks and a .235 average overall in his career over seven seasons with three clubs. But as a player of the harmonica, Linz became one of the most famous accidental motivators in baseball history.

Linz's exploits were reported widely at the time and then immortalized by Jim Bouton in the pitcher's breakthrough rebel book, *Ball Four.* He had labored his way through the Yanks' minor-league system, waiting for his chance behind the regular shortstop, Tony Kubek, and then Tom Tresh, before he was finally promoted as the backup infielder when Kubek left for military service in 1962. The signature harmonica incident took place in Chicago on August 20, 1964, on the team bus returning from a 5–0 drubbing by the White Sox. The Yanks were in the midst of a six-game losing streak, and the defeat dropped their record to 69-50, four and a half games behind Chicago and four behind Baltimore. Linz was sitting in the back of the bus, playing a lilting, irreverent interpretation of "Mary Had a Little Lamb" on the instrument. Yogi Berra was in his first year as manager of the team, and there was already considerable talk that he was too close to his former teammates and was losing control of the club. The Yanks, after all, had won fourteen of the previous seventeen American League pennants and were expected to continue that incredible streak indefinitely.

Berra turned around on the bus and screamed at Linz, "Put that thing in your pocket." Linz kept playing. Berra screamed again. "If you don't knock it off, I'm going to come back there and kick your ass." Linz couldn't hear Berra and asked Mickey Mantle, sitting nearby, what the manager said. "He said to play it louder," said Mantle, forever the prankster. Berra rushed back toward Linz and, according to the Associated Press, yelled, "I told you to put it away. You'd think you'd just won four straight." Linz freaked out at the sight of the usually mild-mannered Berra storming down the bus aisle, knocking the harmonica out of Linz's hands. The instrument struck Joe Pepitone's knee, cutting it.

"Why are you getting on me?" Linz asked Berra. "I give a hundred percent out on the field. I try to win. I should be allowed to do what I want off the field."

Berra replied, "Play it in your room."

The incident is given great credit for the Yanks' turnaround that season, though in reality they dropped the next game 7–0 to the White Sox and also lost the series finale to fall six and a half games back. After that, however, the Yanks went on a 30-11 tear to finish 99-63, beating out the White Sox by a single game. Whether Berra's demonstration of ire had anything to do with that surge is debatable. Just as likely, the story contributed to Berra's unfair dismissal after the Yankees later lost a seven-game World Series to St. Louis. Years later, Berra couldn't say one way or another. The team was in the process of being sold to CBS for $11.2 million, the sale was pending, and the front office's decision-making process was indecipherable.

As for Linz, he came to symbolize the demise of the Yankees' dynasty at this time. He started at shortstop during that 1964 World Series in place of Tony Kubek, who had injured his back. The double-play combination of Linz and Bobby Richardson did not click, and Linz batted .226 in the Series against the Cards—though he did, surprisingly, hit two homers, one of them in Game 7.

Linz earned all of $14,000 for that 1964 season, then hung on with the Yanks for one more year before he was traded to the Phillies for Rubén Amaro. He returned to New York for two seasons with the Mets, averaging .208. He never lost his sense of humor about the harmonica incident. In fact, he made enough money off speaking engagements to open four restaurants, then went into insurance. Berra, always good-natured, embraced the silly moment. Weeks after the event, he posed for a promotional photograph with Linz. The manager was holding his hands over his ears while Linz played his harmonica. More than four decades later, Linz was a regular at Berra's charity golf tournaments. "Yogi never held it against me," he said in one 2005 interview with BaseballSavvy.com. "All my jobs have been because of that. People remember me because of that one incident. I only hit eleven home runs in my whole career, you know, but I'm in all the books."

AL WEIS, THE MOUSE THAT ROARED—FOR A WEEK

Every marginal professional baseball player should be as fortunate as Al Weis and experience just a few glorious moments during an otherwise ho-hum career. Weis not only enjoyed one week of irrational, unprecedented success; he did so at a magical time in history—during the Amazin' Mets' 1969 World Series victory.

Nobody except the supportive manager Gil Hodges could possibly have prophesied Weis's astounding offensive emergence in that series. Until that October, and then again afterward, Weis was a chronically terrible hitter, a utility infielder expected to play little more than a peripheral role on any team. Weis had grown up not too far from Shea Stadium in the Long Island town of Bethpage, then was signed by the White Sox after a stint in the navy. He became a backup for the aging double-play combo of Luis Aparicio and Nellie Fox, briefly filling a starting role at second base in 1963 when the White Sox traded away Fox. Weis was considered a good base stealer and bunter, but he slumped to a truly miserable .155 in 1966 and lost his spot in the lineup. The next season, he collided with Frank Robinson at second base, suffered a fractured leg, and played in only fifty games. He was then dealt to the Mets in what would become a landmark trade—but only because New York also acquired Tommie Agee in the same deal. Reportedly, Hodges insisted on Weis's inclusion in the exchange, because the Mets needed a backup for Bud Harrelson, who was being called up occasionally for military duty. Weis, at a more advanced age of twenty-nine, was immune from such call-ups. He remembered later how he was unhappy about the deal.

"The stumbling, fumbling Mets," Weis recalled. "Going from a pennant contender to a last-place club, you're thinking right away, 'There go my chances of ever playing in the World Series.'"

His debut with the Mets was certainly demoralizing. On April 15, 1968, Weis went 1 for 9 with a walk in a twenty-four-inning game against Houston, a 1–0 loss that remains the longest shutout ever played. He eventually allowed Bob Aspromonte's grounder to zip through his legs in the bottom of the twenty-fourth inning at the Astrodome for an error and the only run of the game. Weis batted .172 in 1968, with one homer in 274 at-bats. He became so discouraged by his persistent slumps that he gave up switch-hitting and began batting only right-handed. Even then, in 1969, he was hitless for April and fighting the .200 mark for much of the season. Hodges, for some reason, never gave up hope in Weis and was rewarded when the Mets improbably caught the Cubs in the regular season, beat the Braves in the National League Championship Series, and made their way into the World Series against the heavily favored Orioles.

Suddenly there was no stopping Weis, who played at least some part in all five Series games. In Game 1, during a 4–1 loss at Memorial Stadium, he drove in the Mets' only run with a sacrifice fly. In Game 2, with the scored tied 1–1 in the top of the ninth, Weis singled home the winning run. Hodges started him at second base in Game 5, batting eighth. The Mets trailed 3–2 in the seventh inning when Weis slammed a leadoff homer—his first homer ever at Shea—against Dave McNally, and the Mets went on to clinch the title behind Jerry Koosman with a 5–3 victory. "When I got near second base," Weis said, "I started hearing the crowd roar and thought something must have happened. I guess I don't know how to react to a home run. I only know how to react to singles and doubles."

Altogether in the World Series, Weis batted .455 (5 for 11) with a homer, three RBIs, four walks, and a .563 on-base percentage. The New York Baseball Writers voted him the Babe Ruth Award for most valuable player in the playoffs, though he was nipped in the national voting for Series MVP by his teammate Donn Clendenon.

His place in Mets history assured, Weis quietly returned to batting .207 in 1970 and was released in July 1971, while he was still hitless in eleven at-bats that season. Altogether, Weis batted .219 with seven homers in ten seasons. His World Series average, however, remained .455 forever.

ELROD HENDRICKS AND THE PHANTOM BASEBALL

Elrod Hendricks really belongs in his own category: a catcher who was so valuable crouched behind the plate that he got away with being terrible whenever he stood beside it with a bat. Hendricks, a Virgin Islands native, persevered through eight years in the minors, batting as low as .211 and .222 for entire seasons. He then lasted a dozen eventful years as a player in the major leagues and another twenty-eight years as a coach, despite averaging just .220 over his career and often skidding below the Mendoza Line. Nonetheless, he became revered in Baltimore as a top defensive catcher, a strong handler of pitchers, and a big part of the Orioles' championship in 1970. At his peak, he was

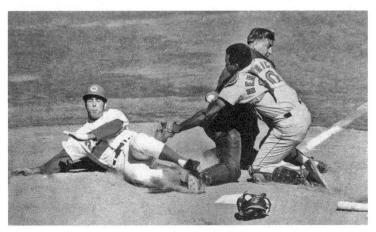

Elrod Hendricks tags out Bernie Carbo with his glove in Game 1 of the 1970 World Series. Somehow, umpire Ken Burkhart never noticed the ball was in Hendricks's other hand. *AP Photo*

throwing out nearly 50 percent of attempted base stealers. In his entire career, Hendricks committed only thirty-one errors and was charged with just fifty-eight passed balls. In fact, he was so good defensively that he once famously didn't require the baseball to make a tag.

That bizarre moment occurred in Game 1 of the 1970 World Series against the Reds. With runners on the corners and one out in the sixth inning, Ty Cline hit a chopper in front of the plate. Hendricks grabbed the ball with his bare hand. He was thinking of throwing to first, but the pitcher, Jim Palmer, screamed at him that the runner Bernie Carbo was storming home from third. Hendricks dived to tag Carbo with his catcher's mitt. Unfortunately, the ball was still clearly in his right hand. No matter. The home plate umpire, Ken Burkhart, didn't really have a great view of the play, because he had collided with Hendricks while looking to see if the batted ball was fair. Burkhart called Carbo out even though there was no legal tag. Meanwhile, Carbo never touched home until he came back to contest the call, stepping on the plate accidentally. The Reds' manager, Sparky Anderson, argued futilely with Burkhart, and the Orioles went on to win that tight first game, 4–3, and then the Series, 4–1.

Earl Weaver loved Hendricks so much in Baltimore the manager kept bringing him back for more. During that championship season of 1970, Hendricks had platooned with Andy Etchebarren on one of the greatest defensive teams in history—including Brooks Robinson at third and Mark Belanger at short-stop. "Defensively, you couldn't find a team that was as good as that ballclub," Hendricks said. "We had Gold Gloves all around the infield. Even though Boog Powell never got credit for being a great first baseman, he saved a lot of errors. And you had Paul Blair in center field, who caught everything."

Actually, Hendricks had three stints with the Orioles. In 1978, at the age of thirty-seven, he was a part-time coach and only played in thirteen games for Baltimore, one of them as a relief pitcher. That oddity happened on June 26, when the Toronto Blue Jays were up, 24–6, in the fifth inning, and Weaver had run out of pitchers. He'd already used an outfielder on the mound, Larry Harlow, who gave up five runs in two-thirds of an inning. Weaver asked Hendricks if he could throw strikes. Hendricks had tossed some batting practice and figured he could do that. "I remember walking in from the bullpen thinking, 'What is the record for most runs in a ballgame?'" he told the Baltimore *Sun*. "My next thought was, 'Don't let them hit it back up the middle.' My whole plan was to throw it inside and hope they pull it. Just throw it as slow as you can, try to mess their timing up. I'd like to say it was fun but it really wasn't." His strategy worked spectacularly. Hendricks pitched two and one-third innings of scoreless, one-hit baseball. A more notable pitcher on that staff, Jim Palmer, got a great kick out of the scene. "The next day we went down to get the papers and there were none left. Elrod had bought them all," Palmer said. The event only made Hendricks more beloved in Baltimore, where he became a mainstay and bullpen coach for twenty-eight years, which meant a franchise-record thirty-seven years in an Orioles uniform. He suffered a stroke in 2005 and died in December of that year from a heart attack, one day shy of sixty-five. Hendricks had become something of an Orioles institution by then, a catcher who didn't even require the baseball to tag out a runner in a World Series game.

NIPPY JONES AND THE SHOE-SHINE INCIDENT

Vernal Leroy "Nippy" Jones was an unremarkable first baseman who always managed to be in the right place at the right time—and that fortunate placement included his left foot. He extended his career with the Cardinals because Stan Musial was being switched from first base to the outfield, leaving a roster spot for Jones. He won World Series with both the Cardinals in 1946 and the Braves in 1957. And though he didn't have much to do with those successful regular seasons, Jones suddenly became the pivotal story line in Milwaukee's seven-game victory over the Yankees.

Jones was picked up by the Braves in mid-season of 1957 after five years of laboring in the minors. He had pinch-hit unsuccessfully twice in Games 1 and 3 of the 1957 World Series, both Milwaukee losses. The Yanks, already ahead two games to one, took a 5–4 lead into the bottom of the tenth inning in Game 4. The Series appeared a foregone conclusion, another Yankee title. Jones led off the inning against Tommy Byrne as a pinch hitter for the Milwaukee ace Warren Spahn. Byrne threw a low pitch that appeared to bounce in the dirt and was called a ball by the home plate umpire, Augie Donatelli. Jones knew differently, however, and went to retrieve the baseball. He showed it to Donatelli, pointing out there was in fact a smudge of black polish on the ball from his left shoe. "That ball hit me!" Jones said. "I mean it! Take a look at the ball." Faced with such indisputable evidence, Donatelli waved Jones to first base while the Yankees' manager, Casey Stengel, stormed about in protest. Byrne was replaced immediately by the reliever Bob Grim. Having done his part, Jones was pulled for the pinch runner Félix Mantilla. Red Schoendienst bunted Mantilla to second, who scored on a double by Johnny Logan. Eddie Mathews slammed a huge, two-run homer to win the game. The Yanks fumed over the shoe-shine incident while the Braves went on to capture the 1957 Series in seven games.

"With all his experience, Byrne probably wouldn't make a pitch like that in a hundred innings, but it happened," Mickey Mantle wrote in a syndicated column the next day. "I guess no Yankee team ever made the flip-flop we did Sunday. We were lifted away up sky high . . . then we hit bottom." After his odd heroics, Jones returned to the minors for three more years before retiring. Eventually, he became a professional fishing guide before dying of a heart attack in 1995 at age seventy. Jones knew where the fish were, just as he knew when his shoe blackened a baseball.

JEFFREY MAIER, BOY SAVIOR

Nearly a decade before Steve Bartman became such an infamous part of Cubs' lore, Jeffrey Maier emerged as a twelve-year-old Yankees superhero by doing more or less the same thing—except his action aided the home team instead of the visitors. Because of that, Maier was celebrated in New York as a champion of great resourcefulness, right alongside Derek Jeter and Bernie Williams.

The incident that thrust Maier into the limelight occurred at Yankee Stadium during the opening game of the American League Championship Series on October 9, 1996, when the Bombers were trailing the Orioles, 4–3, in the bottom of the eighth

Jeffrey Maier reaches over the wall to deflect Derek Jeter's
drive during Game 1 of the 1996 American League Championship
Series. The ball was called a homer and Orioles' right fielder
Tony Tarasco was not amused. *New York* Daily News

inning, Jeter at the plate. The boy had come to the stadium with
friends, fresh off his bar mitzvah, after his mom had written a
white-lie note to the principal of Charles DeWolf Middle School
in Old Tappan, New Jersey, requesting her son be excused from
gym class because of an orthodontist appointment. Maier came
to the game with a black Mizuno mitt, ready for action.

When Jeter came to the plate, Maier remembered how his dad
had told him that Jeter would go to right field against a power
pitcher like Armando Benítez. "I was on high alert," Maier said.
"I was ready to go."

Jeter smacked Benítez's ninety-four-mile-per-hour fastball
deep to right. It wasn't quite going to make the stands. Baltimore's outfielder Tony Tarasco drifted back to the wall, setting
up for the catch, when suddenly Maier descended a few steps
from his front-row perch—section 31, box 325, row A, seat 2. "I
just looked up and stuck my hand out and went for the ball," he
said. Maier deflected the ball back into the seats. By all rights,

this should have elicited a call of spectator interference and either an out or a ground-rule double. Instead, the umpire Rich Garcia gestured that the hit was a home run. Tarasco argued. Davey Johnson, the Orioles' manager, carried on the battle at length and was ejected. There were no replay guidelines in place. Jon Miller, the Baltimore radio man, chronicled the play this way: "Going back is Tarasco, to the warning track, to the wall, he's under it now. . . . It's taken away from him by a fan, and they're gonna call it . . . a home run! I can't believe it. . . . A terrible call by Garcia!"

The homer tied the score, sending the game into extra innings. In the eleventh, Williams slugged a walk-off homer off Randy Myers for the 5–4 victory. The Orioles immediately appealed Garcia's ruling to the American League president, Gene Budig, but a judgment call could not be overturned. The Yanks went on to take the ALCS in five games, then win the World Series against Atlanta, cementing Maier's place in history.

Maier himself became a tremendously popular kid in New York. He was awarded the key to the city by Mayor Rudy Giuliani and made an appearance on the *Late Show with David Letterman*. It turned out he was more than just a baseball dilettante. Maier would go on to pitch and play center field for Northern Valley Regional High School in Old Tappan. He later starred at Wesleyan University, where he became the school's all-time career hits leader and was a first-team selection in the New England Small College Athletic Conference. He appeared at a tryout staged by the Yankees, though that was as far as it got. Far enough, for the Yanks. Maier had become a Yankees legend, alongside the shortstop who struck the homer.

BOTTOM TEN

1   **BRIAN DOYLE**   A gnat with bite.

2   **PHIL LINZ**   Musician to the stars.

3   **AL WEIS**   He repaid Gil Hodges's undeserved faith.

4   **BUCKY DENT**   He batted just .247 for his career, but hit one over the wall in Fenway that changed everything in the 1978 playoff game. Then he batted .417 in the World Series.

5   **ELROD HENDRICKS**   Who needs a baseball to make the tag?

6   **BILL MAZEROSKI**   The Pirates' second baseman smacked only eleven homers during the 1960 regular season, then knocked the walk-off winner to left in Game 7 against the Yanks.

7   **NIPPY JONES**   Polished player.

8   **JEFFREY MAIER**   Tony Tarasco is still looking for the baseball.

9   **JIM SUNDBERG**   The light-hitting catcher went 2 for 4 with four RBIs for the Royals in Game 7 of the 1985 American League Championship Series against the Blue Jays.

10   **DAVID ECKSTEIN**   The five-foot, six-inch shortstop grew twice his size in the postseason. In 2002, he batted .310 in the World Series for the Angels, with nine hits, two walks, and six runs. Then he batted .364 for the Cardinals in the 2006 Series, with four RBIs.

12 | WHEN A ROSE IS NOT A ROSE
Sons and Brothers Who Didn't Cut It

WHEN THE RIGHT sperm hits the right egg, a Pete Rose or Hank Aaron is born into this world. Somehow, foolishly, we often expect the same greatness from close relatives of these baseball geniuses, from their sons, brothers, and cousins. It rarely works that way, unless your name happens to be Griffey, Alou, or Bonds. Genetics is a fussy, elusive science. Most of the time, attempts by children or siblings to follow in the cleats of their kin end in early frustration, in high school careers falling considerably short of the major leagues. Once in a while, a relative will reach the big leagues, step into the spotlight, then fail to live up to his surname. When the acorn falls too far from the tree, the whole world is watching.

PETE JUNIOR: WHEN A ROSE IS NOT A ROSE

Pete Rose Jr. experienced both the great joys and the disadvantages of being the son of . . . well, you know. There was no way to live up to such a should-be-Hall-of-Fame career, yet Pete junior tried his hardest and endured twenty-one seasons in the

With Pete Sr. and Marge Schott watching from the stands, Pete Rose Jr. prepares to bat for the Reds. He wasn't worth the wait. *AP Photo/Al Behrman*

minors—plus an extremely small cup of coffee with the Cincinnati Reds. There was some scandal along the way, too, because Pete was, in this way, certainly his father's son.

Pete junior grew up immersed in the baseball life, hanging out in the dugout as a batboy for his father's clubs and making connections with his dad's teammates. He was everywhere, it seemed, and the TV cameras loved to show him chatting with his dad. In 1982, when Pete senior played all 162 games for the Phillies, the father and twelve-year-old son posed for a Fleer baseball card tagged "Pete & Re-Pete." When Pete senior finally broke Ty Cobb's career record for most hits on September 11, 1985, the teenage Pete junior was there on the field for the celebration.

"I'm as normal as they come," Pete junior would tell MLB.com years later. "The only difference is my dad has more hits than anyone else's dad. That's what it all boils down to." That was no small matter, of course. There were considerable expectations for Pete junior, who was tabbed at age eighteen by the Orioles in the twelfth round of the 1988 draft. But for his first five seasons in the minors with eight different teams, Pete junior never really blossomed. And when he would experience a bad hitting spell, as he did during an 0-for-20 slump during the 1991 season in Sarasota, a phone call to his father for advice didn't help much.

"His response," recalled Pete junior, "was, 'I don't know, son. I've never been in one. Keep swinging. Call me tomorrow.'"

Finally, in 1997, it seemed Pete junior had his left-handed swing together. He batted .308 for Class AA Chattanooga with twenty-five homers, earning a September call-up with the Reds. It probably didn't help that this big opportunity arrived in Cincinnati, of all places, where his father was still celebrated as an immortal. "He's our Babe Ruth in Cincinnati," Pete junior said. The son was not Ruth, not by a long shot. He had two singles in fourteen at-bats and eleven games for the Reds, committing two errors in two games at third base. He finished his major-league career 4,254 hits behind his father.

Still, Pete junior stuck with it and played for a series of minor-league clubs, where he averaged .271 for his career, often with small independent teams in places like Joliet and Newark and with virtually no hope for advancement. "My heart is shaped like a baseball," he said. "I grew up and know the lifestyle and have done this all my life."

Unfortunately, he also inherited some recklessness from his father. Pete junior was indicted and pleaded guilty in November 2005 to a charge of distributing the relaxant drug gamma-Butyrolactone (GBL) to minor-league teammates in the 1990s. He served one month in prison in 2006. Undeterred by this setback, Pete junior immediately returned to playing baseball for the Bridgeport Bluefish upon his release. By 2011, he was finally retired from playing while managing in the White Sox farm system. Nobody, he felt, could better relate to these flawed Class A minor leaguers.

"I've played seven years of 'A' ball, which is kind of unheard-of," Rose junior said. "You tell guys on the bubble, 'What are you going to do? Are you going to quit?' There never was any quit in what I was going to do. I've been released and all the other stuff. You just keep playing and keep scratching and good things will happen." Or not.

TOMMIE AARON, FOREVER LITTLE BROTHER

Tommie Aaron is co-owner of the all-time record for career major-league home runs by brothers—768. Of course, anybody with knowledge of baseball history and basic math can quickly figure out that Tommie contributed only thirteen homers toward that mark, which is not a very impressive total over seven seasons and 944 at-bats.

Hank Aaron was twenty-three years old, coming off his 1957 MVP season with forty-four homers and 132 RBIs, when the Milwaukee Braves understandably decided the next year to sign the star's eighteen-year-old brother to a contract. Tommie was a promising outfielder and first baseman in his own right out of Mobile, Alabama. For the next few years he continued to demonstrate considerable skill and power in the minors, hitting .299 with fifteen homers and seventy RBIs for Class AA Austin of the Texas League in 1961. While nobody thought he would evolve into his brother, there were still considerable expectations afoot. He was promoted to the big club in 1962 and at times played in the same lineup with Hank. Yet he never lived up to the hope or hype. Tommie was used as a utility player, appearing over his career at every position other than pitcher, catcher, and shortstop. He batted .231 with Milwaukee in 1962, then .200 in 1963.

After another encouraging spell in the minors—Tommie was MVP of the International League with Richmond in 1967—his eventual return to the Atlanta Braves proved yet another disappointment. From 1968 to 1971, Tommie's batting average slipped from a high of .250 to .206 and .226. His greatest claim to fame, other than the identity of his brother, was going 5 for 15 lifetime against the great Juan Marichal.

Tommie Aaron's lengthy, up-and-down career always begged the question whether he was given preferential treatment because of his brother or whether he actually had to work harder to earn promotion to the majors. Hank Aaron's brother-in-law, Bill Lucas, who would eventually become the Braves' director of player personnel, thought the deck was stacked against Tommie. "I've always

Hank and Tommie Aaron were brothers and teammates. The similarities ended there.
AP Photo/Paul Shane

said that if his name was Tommie Jones instead of Tommie Aaron he would have gotten a better shot," Lucas said in a 1973 interview with *Sport* magazine. "At Austin once I remember he hit a long home run and as he was circling the bases some fan yelled, 'Hey Tommie, Hank hit two today.' It was always like that."

Tommie and Hank homered a total of three times in the same game in 1962. On June 28, 1965, Tommie, starting in left field, knocked in the winning run with a seventh-inning single in a 4–3 victory over Philadelphia in Atlanta. Earlier in the game, his single had driven home his brother Hank, who was playing right field and homered once. "About time I started hitting," Tommie said afterward. "I think I may be ready to come out of my slump. I just sit back and wait for the man [manager Lum Harris] to call on me. That's all I can do, but I have to be ready." Tommie and Hank both appeared in the 1969 National League Championship Series against the Mets—sort of. Hank batted .357, with three homers. Tommie was 0 for 1.

Though the two brothers were teammates, they weren't particularly close until Tommie's playing days were done and he became a manager in the minors and then a coach with the Braves in Atlanta. Tommie contracted leukemia, which was diagnosed in 1982 by Braves' team physicians during routine tests. He died at age forty-five in 1984. At the time, he was serving in his sixth season as an Atlanta coach, while his brother had been retired for eight years. Until the farm team moved to Gwinnett County, Georgia, in 2008, the Richmond Braves handed out the Tommie Aaron Memorial Award to the club's most valuable player, and his uniform number 23 was retired. "Hell, not everyone can be Hank Aaron," Tommie Aaron once said, on his way to a career .229 batting average. "That guy is unique in the world."

TODD HUNDLEY, THE SON ALSO CROUCHES

Cubs fans love to wallow in the vastness of their franchise's unending failure. And there is nothing more romantic than the lore of 1969, when a very good Chicago team blew a large lead to the Amazin' Mets, who happened to have much better pitching. Some of those Cubbie names—Ernie Banks, Glenn Beckert, Don Kessinger, Ron Santo, Billy Williams, and Randy Hundley—still evoke the welling of tears around Wrigleyville. Hundley was always viewed as the grit and glue of that team. He was a decent clutch hitter and a truly special defensive catcher who threw out 50 percent of base stealers during his prime. So when his son, Todd (born in 1969, by the way), became available after the 2000 season, the Cubs threw money at him while hoping the son would demonstrate the same scrappy leadership. They had reason to believe this was true, beyond nostalgia. Todd Hundley had once set a record for homers by a catcher, forty-one, with the Mets in 1996, while catching 150 games that season. Shoulder surgery at the end of the next season impacted his throwing. He didn't own his dad's arm—he nailed only about 25 percent of runners—but had batted .284 with twenty-four homers in pitcher-friendly Dodger Stadium. Imagine what he would do at cozy Wrigley Field.

Todd Hundley received a four-year, $23.5 million deal from the Cubs and promptly fell apart. His stats in 2001 were a catastrophe. Hundley batted .187 and struck out eighty-nine times in only 246 at-bats while throwing out just 20 percent of base stealers. The numbers didn't get much better the next year, when he hit .211. He also was at war with Cubs fans and with the manager, Don Baylor.

On June 26, 2002, in a game at Wrigley Field against the Reds, Hundley hit a home run and showed his middle finger to spectators while he rounded the bases. He later claimed the gesture was aimed at a small group of Reds fans, but few Chicagoans accepted this explanation. Baylor, meanwhile, lost his job less than two weeks later, in some part because of Hundley's ineffectiveness. Baylor preferred to use Joe Girardi at catcher whenever possible and often cited hot weather during the summer as his public excuse for resting Hundley. Baylor said Hundley sweated so much he became dehydrated during the Cubs' many day games. "He goes through . . . a shirt an inning," Baylor said. For Hundley, these unaccustomed benchings were an embarrassment—particularly in Chicago, where his dad caught 160 games in 1968. After Baylor was dismissed, Todd Hundley exploded.

"The heat was never an issue, but this guy made it an issue," he said. "Look, do you honestly think I wasn't playing because of the heat? I've caught more than a thousand games, more than five hundred in ninety-degree-plus conditions. But I couldn't say nothing. All the time, it was like talking to a wall."

At this juncture, foolishly, the Dodgers thought Hundley might rekindle his career if he returned to Los Angeles. They rescued the Cubs from the remaining $13.5 million on his contract, dealing Mark Grudzielanek and Eric Karros to Chicago. On the clubs' payroll sheets, this was more or less a wash. Grudzielanek would be getting $5.5 million in 2003, while Karros was set to receive $8.375 million. But Grudzielanek was a fine second baseman who batted over .300 for the Cubs in each of the next two seasons. Meanwhile, Hundley failed to revive his career in Los Angeles and ripped Cubs fans from afar. He spent most of 2003 on the disabled list with a bad back. After a second surgery to repair a herniated disk, he didn't show up for training camp and didn't play a single game in 2004, the final year of his contract.

As if Todd Hundley required an unhappy coda to his career, he was cited in the 2007 *Mitchell Report* for using performance-enhancing drugs. The report stated that Hundley first received steroids while he was with the Mets from the clubhouse attendant Kirk Radomski in the mid-1990s. The report also stated Hundley introduced several Dodgers players to Radomski and that they became involved in steroids. While there was no indication he continued this habit in Chicago, Todd Hundley's legacy with the Cubs in no shape or form resembled his father's golden memories.

RICH MURRAY AND THE GIANT FOOTSTEPS

It was bad enough being Eddie Murray's little brother, but poor Rich Murray didn't have only those large shoes to fill. After a series of weird events in 1980, he was suddenly supposed to take over at first base for Willie McCovey, arguably the most popular San Francisco Giant in history. Murray was just twenty-two at the time, having been drafted in the sixth round by the Giants in 1975 out of Locke High School in Los Angeles. He had some modest success in the minors and was promoted to back up the aging McCovey and the veteran Mike Ivie at first base.

Then, suddenly, Ivie retired, out of nowhere, at age twenty-seven, after taking time off for an injury to his finger and then for mental exhaustion. "The big leagues aren't all they're cracked up to be," Ivie said, proclaiming regret he never went to college. "It's a super big decision. I'm going to leave a lot of money. I'm ready to look for something else. Nobody's going to talk me out of this." McCovey had announced his own plans for retiring in July—he only wanted to be able to play in four different decades—and was viewed more as a pinch hitter than anything. The job of first baseman on the struggling San Francisco Giants had fallen into the lap of Murray.

Murray did his best, but it clearly wasn't enough. Wholly unprepared for this responsibility, he batted .216 with four homers and twenty-four RBIs in fifty-three games and 194 at-bats in 1980. After a strong start he went 2 for 23 in late June and was replaced by Ivie, who came out of retirement quickly enough. The Giants did Murray no favors. They demoted him to the minors, where he performed well enough. He was picked up by the Indians and the Expos, re-signed by the Giants, and brought up again for one last cup of coffee in June 1983, when he went 2 for 10. This left Rich Murray with 44 hits and four homers in the majors, or 3,211 hits and five hundred homers shy of Eddie's totals. After Eddie was traded from the Orioles to the Dodgers in 1988, he was asked whether he would take special pleasure in beating the Giants because they had not treated his brother well. "I didn't think he got a fair deal," Eddie Murray said. "But I don't think about that when I play the Giants."

BIG RED MACHINE, LITTLE RED GIZMO

Eduardo Pérez earned $1.75 million in his final season, 2006, when he ended his career in the major leagues with an 8-for-51 slump for the Seattle Mariners. He played in a hundred games or more during only two seasons in the major leagues with six teams—not counting a spell in Japan. No matter. Pérez went on to become an ESPN analyst for several years on *Baseball Tonight* and then was hired in 2011 as batting coach for the Florida Marlins. He became yet another hitting expert whose credentials—a .247 career batting average with just seventy-nine homers in thirteen years—hardly seemed to justify the title. By comparison, his dad, Tony, made only $225,000 while hitting .328 for Cincinnati at the tail end of a Hall of Fame career. Tony wasn't hired as a broadcaster and was fired after a run of only forty-four games as manager of the Reds in 1993.

Life isn't fair, and Eduardo Pérez was well aware of its fickle nature. He was a top prospect out of Florida State, where he batted .377 as a senior and led the team into the College World Series. Picked by the Angels in the first round of the 1991 draft, Eduardo showed considerable promise in the minors. In 1993, he batted .306 with seventy RBIs in ninety-six games for Triple-A Vancouver of the Pacific Coast League. Called up by the Angels in July, he batted .290 over his first eighteen games before a 4-for-34 stretch brought him back to earth. He never recovered his stroke or his equilibrium. Pérez batted .209, .169, and .222 over the next three seasons with California and Cincinnati, where it was hoped he might bring back memories of Tony—the one person who retained a level head on all this. "I got him and took him to the side and said, 'You are Eduardo Pérez,'" Tony Pérez said. "Never try to be like me. Be yourself. Nobody is trying to push you."

Eduardo enjoyed one moment of glory, knocking a pinch

homer in the 2002 National League Championship Series for St. Louis against the Giants. Eventually, he found himself at age thirty-six on the Mariners, a serendipitous landing spot. Five sons of the Big Red Machine from the 1970s were drafted in the first round by major-league teams, and three of them played in Seattle—Pérez, Ken Griffey Jr., and Ed Sprague Jr. "I just think there's a lot of sons of major leaguers out there who have something to contribute to the game," Eduardo Pérez said. "My dad was a great player, a great baseball man. I still just keep picking his brain for knowledge."

Tony couldn't impart his Hall of Fame batting skills to Eduardo, but there were some nuances to the game more easily taught. Eduardo won one game for Seattle by forcing a tie-breaking, two-base error from the Boston shortstop Alex González. Running from second to third on the play, Eduardo didn't slide into the bag. "I was taught you just don't slide in that situation, to make it a tougher throw," he said. He learned that from his dad. And then Tony Pérez, as assistant to the president of the Marlins, wielded some influence in getting his son the job as batting coach in Florida. Even Eduardo felt a bit self-conscious about the appointment.

"A lot of people just see me as a face with a lot of makeup on *Baseball Tonight*," he said after the appointment. "But [coaching] has definitely been a passion of mine." If Eduardo develops even one Tony Pérez, he will have done just fine.

BOTTOM TEN

1   **PETE ROSE JR.**   Baseball lifer with just two singles to show for it.

2   **TOMMIE AARON**   Only 742 homers behind his big brother.

3   **TODD HUNDLEY**   Cubs mistook him for Randy and paid the price.

4   **EARLE MACK**   Won forty-five games managing the Athletics over two seasons. His father, Connie, won nine pennants and five World Series as a manager.

5   **RICH MURRAY**   Couldn't hit like Eddie, couldn't replace Willie McCovey.

6   **TIM RAINES JR.**   His dad led the league in batting in 1986 and was a seven-time All-Star. Junior hit .213 during his three-season career.

7   **EDUARDO PÉREZ**   Made more money than his dad, Tony, even if he didn't deserve it.

8   **JEREMY GIAMBI**   Hit only 52 homers—377 fewer than Jason—and was nailed at the plate on Derek Jeter's shovel pass because he didn't slide.

9   **BILLY RIPKEN**   Forever in Cal junior's shadow—even when they both played for their father in 1987.

10   **WILTON GUERRERO**   Didn't look like his younger brother Vlad, and certainly didn't hit like him.

13 THE PHOLD
The Worst Managers Ever

NOT EVERYBODY IS a born leader, or even a decent student of the game. Great players often make bad managers. Bad players can make bad managers, too. Quiet introverts or in-your-face screamers may press all the wrong buttons, follow all the wrong hunches. A few bad losses may turn the clubhouse against the leader. As Casey Stengel once said, "The secret of managing is to keep the guys who hate you away from the guys who are undecided." Not everyone is good at that, either. It's tough to figure out in advance whether a man is managerial material, whether he'll earn the respect of the clubhouse. When Joe Torre was hired to take over the Yankees in 1996, the headline in the New York *Daily News* read, "Clueless Joe." That was just before he won four titles in five years. Then there were the managers who arrived with high expectations and left with hopelessly low win totals or disappointing finishes.

GENE MAUCH AND THE PHOLD

What, exactly, makes for a lousy manager? If it is someone who just can't quite get a very good team over the top, who can never capture the big one, then Gene Mauch is the perfect paradigm. Mauch won 1,902 games, the eighth-highest total in major-league history, with four teams over twenty-six seasons from 1960 to 1987. Yet he also lost 2,037 games, some of them heartbreaking,

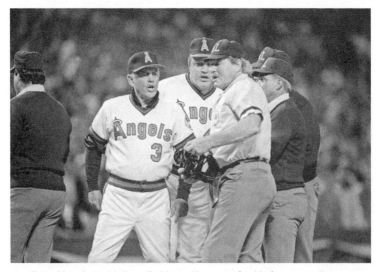

Gene Mauch couldn't really blame the umps for his famous collapses while managing the Phillies and Angels. *AP Photo*

and never, ever advanced to the World Series. On three occasions, Mauch came within a single game of reaching that goal, and each time his side came crashing down in spectacular fashion. He will always be remembered most for the collapse of 1964, when he managed the Phillies, panic-style, into what would forever be referred to as "the Phold."

That year, the Phils were coasting to a National League title at 90-60, six and a half games up with a dozen games remaining—the first seven of those at home. Somehow, they dropped ten straight and blew the pennant to the Cardinals. Mauch was always known as a small-ball manager, preferring defense and the stolen base to the home run, but on that team he had two substantial power hitters in Johnny Callison and Rookie of the

Year Richie Allen, who combined for sixty homers. Mauch also had two aces, Jim Bunning and Chris Short, and a closer of sorts in the bullpen, Jack Baldschun. He was all set up, it seemed, and then suddenly he wasn't.

"We even started buying World Series tickets," Dallas Green, a relief pitcher on that team, told Fox Sports. "I still have a couple of them around the house somewhere." The Phils started their bad stretch by losing to the Reds, 1–0, when Chico Ruiz unpredictably stole home with the slugger Frank Robinson at the plate. It made no sense whatsoever. Hoping to end the race before it grew too tight, Mauch started Short and Bunning on just two days' rest on six occasions. They started seven of the last ten games altogether, and the Phils just kept losing. That wasn't the only problem, though. Mauch was mad for some reason at Baldschun, wouldn't use him much anymore, and the bullpen kept blowing games late. "Once you got in Gene's doghouse, you never got out," Green said. The Phils frittered away a 4–0 lead to the Braves on September 26, when Mauch pulled Baldschun early for Bobby Shantz. The streak kept growing, and Mauch was visibly affected. Normally a screamer, he became eerily quiet. By the time the Phils won their last two games, it was too late. They finished in a second-place tie with the Reds, one game behind St. Louis. "Losing streaks are funny," Mauch said. "If you lose at the beginning you got off to a bad start. If you lose in the middle of the season, you're in a slump. If you lose at the end, you're choking." Mauch knew a lot about losing streaks. His 1961 Phils had dropped twenty-three in a row, and his 1969 Expos would lose twenty straight.

The Phold would not be the last frustrating dance for Mauch, not by a long shot. In 1982, he won the American League's Western Division with the Angels, who then captured the first two games over the Milwaukee Brewers in a best-of-five American League Championship Series. Mauch proved, however, to have learned little from his own history, starting Tommy John and

Bruce Kison in Games 4 and 5 on just three days' rest. John was hammered in Game 4, and then the Brewers won a tough, 4–3 decider. The Angels were one strike away from winning the best-of-five ALCS against the Red Sox in 1986 when Dave Henderson slammed a homer off the reliever Donnie Moore and the Red Sox went on to win in extra innings. Asked if he was still proud of his team's accomplishments, Mauch quipped, "You have to bear in mind that Mr. Autry's favorite horse was named Champion. He ain't ever had one called Runner Up."

STUMP MERRILL AND THE UNLIKELY ART OF LOSING WITH THE YANKEES

Hard to believe now, but for the first and only time in their history the mighty New York Yankees strung together four successive losing seasons from 1989 to 1992. Fairly or not, Stump Merrill became the very personification of that slump after taking over from the popular Bucky Dent as manager on June 6, 1990—coincidentally, two days before the Yanks picked Andy Pettitte and Jorge Posada in the major-league draft and set their eventual comeback in motion.

Dent, of course, won a pennant for the Yanks with a homer in Fenway Park. George Steinbrenner had the gall to fire him right before a scheduled game in Boston, endearing the owner to nobody. Steinbrenner was unable to bring back his go-to sub, Billy Martin, who had died the previous winter in an auto accident. So he settled on Merrill, forty-six years old at the time, a former minor-league nonentity and an organization guy through and through who had managed an assortment of Yankee farm clubs with some success. He'd been tagged with the nickname Stump by a coach when the five-foot, eight-inch Merrill was playing minor-league ball in Maine, walking alongside two taller teammates, and after the coach tried in vain to get his attention.

"My main concern," Merrill said upon word of his promotion, "is to get them playing and having fun. I'm not saying anything against Bucky but, from watching them, it looked like a listless ball club from what I saw."

There wasn't much fun to be had, just a lot of losing. Steinbrenner had been typically impatient with Dent, but he quickly became embroiled in other matters that would occupy his attention, getting himself banned from baseball on July 30, 1990, for his role in hiring a personal investigator, Howie Spira, to besmirch Dave Winfield's reputation. It was Merrill's good fortune to be hired just seven weeks before this ban, allowing him to retain his job despite considerably more losing than any other manager during Steinbrenner's iron reign. It was Merrill's bad fortune, however, to be placed in charge of this team in transition and utter chaos.

There was something of a circus atmosphere to this Yankees side. Winfield was angry and gone, traded to the Angels in May. Don Mattingly would miss much of the season with a back problem. The Yanks had drafted wacky Deion Sanders, who was not doing well, and signed the free-agent failure Andy Hawkins to a large contract. Clearly, the uninspiring Merrill with the unfortunate nickname was not about to turn around this *Titanic*. The Yankees dropped their first four games after Merrill was named manager and just kept losing. Silly, embarrassing things kept happening. Hawkins finally had a good outing and lost a no-hitter to Chicago by the one-sided score of 4–0 because of a bases-loaded, base-clearing error by the outfielder Jim Leyritz. Less than two weeks later, Hawkins and the Yanks were no-hit in a six-inning, rain-shortened game against the same White Sox. After much nonsense, the Yanks finished at 67-95, the worst record in the American League and dead last, seventh place, in the American League East.

Primarily because of Steinbrenner's inability to meddle in the day-to-day operations, Merrill was retained for the 1991 season. The Yanks improved, slightly, to 71-91, finishing fifth, though matters only grew worse, in a manner of speaking. In mid-August, Merrill foolishly benched Don Mattingly, batting .305 at the time, because his hair was too shaggy, fining the Hit Man $250 plus $100 for each day he failed to cut his locks. With this act, Merrill completely lost the clubhouse. *The New York Times* quoted one unidentified player who wanted the media to demand Stump's scalp. "It's your fault," the player told reporters. "Where is the rabid New York media of the last three years? The guy doesn't even know strategy. Anyone who knows baseball can see that."

Merrill was mercifully fired on October 7, 1991, after posting a 120-155 (.436) mark with the most successful franchise in professional sports.

LEE ELIA AND THE TIRADE

Baseball managers are faced with three basic rules for survival: Don't knock your superstars. Don't knock your owners. Don't knock your fans, who happen to be the people who pay the owners, who then pay the superstars. For some reason, Lee Elia ignored this third and arguably most important rule. His rant on April 29, 1983, would become the gold standard for self-immolation.

Elia was just starting out on his second season with the Cubs after being brought over from the Phillies' organization by the general manager, Dallas Green. The Cubs were off to a brutal start—even by Cubs standards—at 5-13. Then they lost again by a run, at home, to the Dodgers, and the fans were merciless. The games at Wrigley Field, which had no lights at the time, were all played during the day, and this fact offered Elia a theme to his tirade: Cubs fans, in his eyes, on this day, were lazy bums. Only he didn't say bums.

"I'll tell you one fuckin' thing," Elia started.

I hope we get fuckin' hotter than shit just to stuff it up them three thousand fuckin' people that show up every fuckin' day. Because if they're the real Chicago fuckin' fans, they can kiss my fuckin' ass, right downtown, and print it! They're really, really behind you around here [note: sarcastic tone]. My fuckin' ass! What the fuck am I supposed to do? Go out there and get destroyed and be quiet about it? For the fuckin' nickel-dime people that show up? The mother-fuckers don't even work! That's why they're out at the fuckin' game! They ought to get a fuckin' job and find out what it's like to go out and earn a fuckin' living. Eighty-five percent of the fuckin' world is working. The other fifteen come out here. A fuckin' play-ground for the cocksuckers. Rip them motherfuckers! Rip those cocksuckers, like the fuckin' people boo. And that's the Cubs? My fuckin' ass! They talk about the great fuckin' support that the players get around here. I haven't seen it this fuckin' year!

Lee Elia throws another tantrum— this one wisely aimed at an umpire, instead of at the Wrigley Field faithful. *AP Photo/Jon Swart*

Elia said all this in the manager's office. In today's world, his speech would have been tweeted immediately in 140-character spurts and likely shown live on the team's own network during a postgame telecast. Back in 1983, however, there were only four reporters hearing this, and only Les Grobstein of WLS-AM radio had an audiotape of Elia's meltdown. "Les called me on the studio hot line and says, 'Tommy, Lee Elia went bonkers and I got it all on tape—I'm bringing it in,'" remembered Tommy Edwards of the station in an interview with the Chicago *Reader*. "I promoed it on the air and he fed it to the newsroom. We bleeped the obscenities and then we ran it. It became a classic."

Grobstein continued to play the tape for many years to come. Elia might have survived his tantrum about the fans' lack of loyalty under different circumstances. Other coaches and managers have done so. But when he basically called them unemployed louses for showing up at day games, he was attacking his only spectator base. Plus, his record with the Cubs was horrid. He became a dead man managing and was fired on August 21 when the Cubs were 54-69 and in fifth place. The Cubbies did just fine without him. This was the Ryne Sandberg era, after all, and the club came within one victory of the World Series in 1984. Meanwhile, as indisputable proof of the old boys' network, Elia received many more opportunities in baseball. He was named manager of the Phillies in 1987 and was fired just before the close of the 1988 season after "leading" the team to a 60-92 mark. His final managerial record was 238-300, with no finish better than fourth place. Elia somehow continued to be inundated with various job offers from the Phillies, the Mariners, and the Dodgers. He hadn't insulted management, after all. Just the fans.

ROY HARTSFIELD, WRONG PLACE AT THE WRONG TIME

Nobody said being a baseball manager was easy, or even remotely fair. By every indication, Roy Hartsfield was a competent fellow who had enjoyed considerable success managing in Spokane and Hawaii at the top levels of minor-league baseball. When Toronto was granted a major-league franchise during the 1977 expansion, the general manager, Peter Bavasi, picked Hartsfield as the club's first manager because the two had worked together for years in the Dodger organization. Hartsfield reminded Bavasi of quiet, steady Walter Alston. "Roy Hartsfield," Bavasi once told his dad, the Dodgers' vice president Buzzie Bavasi, before a torrent of defeats, "is the best manager in baseball."

There are only a handful of managerial openings every year, and Hartsfield was thrilled to get this opportunity. But really, he was doomed from the start. The Blue Jays' roster was a collection of nobodies. Not a single player earned as much as $100,000 that first season, and about the most famous name on the team was Ron Fairly, the longtime Dodgers player who was by then a thirty-nine-year-old designated hitter. The Jays won their inaugural game that season at Exhibition Stadium, 9–5, on a field ringed with snow, but went 54-107 and finished in last place their first season, forty-five and a half games behind the Yanks, no great surprise. The Red Sox knocked seven solo homers off Hartsfield's pitchers on July 4, a major-league record. The other historically notable occurrence was a deliberate forfeit by the Orioles' manager, Earl Weaver, who pulled his team off the field in the fifth inning after arguing with the umpire Marty Springstead that a tarp on the bullpen mound was a risk to his relievers. The Blue Jays were awarded a 9–0 victory, accounting for one fifty-fourth of their win total. Hartsfield was retained for two more years. There were no signs of improvement in 1978 or 1979, when the Jays went 59-102 and then dipped to 53-109. Altogether, Hartsfield's teams had gone 166-318 for a .343 winning percentage—the lowest, to this date, of any manager since 1970 with that kind of relatively lengthy tenure.

"When you're in on the ground floor of something new, you'd like to be around in some capacity to reap some benefits," Hartsfield said later. "They don't keep the first manager around. That's not a kick at anybody. That's just the way it unfortunately happens. I was enthused, quite happy about the way we competed. We lost a lot of games, but we were in a lot of games. It was kind of thrilling for me. But in the last year, it was sort of like a holding pattern. We didn't see a great deal of improvement in the ball club because we didn't make any changes. You were waiting for something to happen, but it didn't happen."

Toward the end, it got ugly—as losing often does. Hartsfield threw his lot in with younger players, generously sacrificing his own career to build something for the future. Tom Buskey, a relief pitcher, said Hartsfield should be fired, and he was backed up by veterans like Roy Howell, Tom Underwood, and Rick Bosetti. Hartsfield was also viewed as an ally of Peter Bavasi's, and then Bavasi made a wisecrack to a reporter: "I would never let my daughter date a Blue Jays player." Howell, who was a player rep on the team, bristled at that one. "How do you think our wives feel about that remark? They married one."

The losing clearly was not all Hartsfield's fault, and that was proved soon enough. He was replaced by Bobby Mattick, who almost impossibly managed to finish in last place three times with Toronto over the next two seasons and to become a great answer to a trivia question: the Jays finished last in both halves of the strike-ridden 1981 season. Hartsfield was just fifty-four when he was dismissed as manager and was never afforded an opportunity with another, better-equipped side. He cherished one experience, though: Hartsfield was named to the 1979 All-Star Game coaching staff, a highlight. He was married to the same woman for sixty years and died of liver cancer on January 15, 2011, at the age of eighty-five. Among the quotes attributed to Hartsfield was one about how he always wanted to work for anything he received. "I do not want someone to give me the finger," he said. "I want to earn it."

JIMMY DYKES'S VERY LONG CAREER

By all accounts, Jimmy Dykes was a nice man and a wonderful infielder during his abundant playing days. He also suffered greatly for several decades with losing teams as a manager,
leading him to comment wistfully, "When you're winning, beer
tastes better." Dykes's futility officially reached legendary status
in mid-season 1960, when he was traded as manager from one
losing team, Detroit, to another bad one, Cleveland.

Dykes was a baseball lifer, playing semi-professionally in
Philadelphia from the age of sixteen. He batted over .300 for five
of his fifteen seasons with the Philadelphia Athletics and was
still batting over .300 as a utility player with the White Sox in
his early forties. At his peak in 1929 and 1930, starting at several
infield positions for the manager Connie Mack, Dykes helped
the A's beat Babe Ruth's Yankees during the regular season and
then win titles with his strong batting performances in the 1929
and 1930 World Series. He had decent power and, according
to Mack, "the best throwing arm in my infield." In retrospect,
Dykes probably deserved better than the high-water mark of
10 percent support he received from baseball writers in Hall of
Fame balloting.

Toward the end of his playing career, early in the 1934 season, he became that oddest and most impractical of hybrids, a
player-manager for the White Sox. He attempted these dual
roles for parts of six seasons, inserting himself in the lineup
with decreasing frequency. There was a lot to be said for Dykes
the player. Unfortunately, he was also one of the most consistently losing managers in history, enduring twenty-one seasons
without a single division title and never finishing higher than
third place. His longevity in the dugout was remarkable, really,
a testimony to his popularity with players and employers, even
as he posted losing records in thirteen of his seasons managing

An impatient skipper in the dugout, Jimmy Dykes was somehow traded as manager in mid-season of 1960 from the Tigers to the Indians. *AP Photo*

the White Sox, Athletics, Orioles, Redlegs, Tigers, and Indians. Dykes gainfully managed mediocre or downright lousy teams during a span from 1934 to 1961, often instructing players far less gifted than himself. He found it difficult to part ways with even the worst of them. "The manager's toughest job," Dykes once said, "is not calling the right play with the bases full and the score tied in an extra-inning game. It's telling a ballplayer that he's through, done, finished."

Dykes also found that it was far more difficult to sit in a dugout than it was to play the game. His temper flared often, at umpires and sometimes at his own players. When one of his batters, Zeke Bonura, kept missing signs, Dykes finally screamed out, "Bunt, you meathead! Bunt! Bunt! B-U-N-T!"

Dykes's run-ins with umps became legendary and statistically impressive. The research of one journalist, Don McKean, found that Dykes was ejected from sixty-two games and suspended thirty-seven times. On July 6, 1941, the American League's president, Will Harridge, handed down a suspension to Dykes "for his conduct and language to umpire Steve Basil. . . . He will remain suspended until he can satisfy the American League office that in the future he will fall in line with the other seven managers of the league in conducting himself and his ball club." The suspension lasted only one week, thanks in part to the lobbying of the White Sox owner, Grace Comiskey.

Despite all the losing, Dykes was considered an innovative sort. He decided to pitch the aging veteran Ted Lyons only once a week, on Sundays, to rest Lyons's arm and to draw fans to watch the popular player. Lyons responded spectacularly, leading the league with a 2.10 ERA in 1942. Dykes might have been considerably more famous, however, if he'd had the nerve to follow his instincts. When the White Sox played an exhibition game in March 1938 against a local team from Pasadena, Dykes spotted a talented African-American player and said, "Geez, if that kid was white, I'd sign him right now." Four years later, Dykes actually invited that player and another black prospect, Nate Moreland, to try out for the White Sox. He never signed either one, however, or we might be speaking of Dykes today in the same reverential tones reserved for Branch Rickey.

Dykes was hired by his old mentor, Mack, to manage in Philadelphia. Later, when he was struggling in Detroit, Cleveland's general manager, Frank Lane, initiated a deal with the Tigers that sent Cleveland's manager, Joe Gordon, to Detroit in exchange for Dykes. The wacky trade failed all around. Detroit remained mired in sixth place, while Cleveland finished fourth on the way to fifth in 1961. That, finally, was the end of Dykes's managerial career, though he would coach in Milwaukee and Kansas City and broadcast Phillies games on the radio. Dykes spent virtually his entire post-playing life around a baseball diamond, finding satisfaction somehow in all the losing.

DON WAKAMATSU AND THE STEEP DESCENT

There was a lot of pressure in 2010 on Don Wakamatsu, for a lot of reasons. The Seattle manager was the first Asian-American manager in the history of Major League Baseball when he was hired to lead the Mariners one year earlier. Seattle already owned the most famous Japanese baseball player, Ichiro Suzuki, and had an enormous following in his home country. Many eyes were watching. Wakamatsu also created his own great expectations after leading the club to a surprising 85-77 record in his debut season—an improvement of twenty-four games from 2008. The Mariners, encouraged by those results, uncharacteristically took on a $9 million salary by trading for Cliff Lee and a bloated $11 million salary by acquiring the outfielder Milton Bradley. They signed the free-agent speedster Chone Figgins to a four-year, $36 million deal. With Lee and the young ace Félix Hernández in the rotation, it figured that Seattle would make a real run at the playoffs for the first time in nine years. Instead, that 2010 season became one of the most nightmarish experiences in recent baseball history, and Wakamatsu never made it out of August. Perhaps because of his personal background, Wakamatsu was always a feisty, fiery type on the field and in the clubhouse, often getting into heated arguments with his own players. He had a mixed-race heritage and a sense of history. His father was born in a Japanese-American internment camp, the Tule Lake War Relocation Center in Northern California. His grandparents actually bought the barracks where they had been assigned during World War II and remained there to raise their family.

"How ironic," Wakamatsu told the *San Francisco Chronicle*. "They had forty-eight hours to relocate, they were imprisoned for years and they chose to live the rest of their lives in the same buildings."

He was the last pick of the New York Yankees in the 1984 draft and played catcher briefly for the White Sox in 1991. Wakamatsu was charged with two passed balls in his first game, trying to catch the knuckleballer Charlie Hough. He later became a bench coach in Texas before taking over in Seattle from the interim manager Jim Riggleman. That first season was a dream. The chronically woeful Mariners performed beyond all expectations, and Wakamatsu was selected as a coach during the 2009 All-Star Game.

Disaster followed, and it included a collective emotional meltdown. It is truly rare for so many quality players to have career-low seasons, particularly on offense, and Wakamatsu's temper did not serve him well under such circumstances. Wakamatsu sent Milton Bradley home from one game in May, and then Bradley (who finished the season batting .205) sought counseling for two weeks. The manager benched the local hero Ken Griffey Jr. in early June, when Griffey's average hit the skids at .184. Griffey headed to his home in Florida and announced his retirement from there, embarrassing the organization. Figgins's batting average dipped to .259, and he had several public spats with Wakamatsu. Then, a final embarrassment: during a home game, Wakamatsu got into a shoving and shouting match in the dugout with his infielder José López, pulling the player's jersey over his back, hockey-style. When Wakamatsu was finally fired, along with his bench coach Ty Van Burkleo and pitching coach Rick Adair, the Mariners were the worst hitting team in baseball, falling to 42-70 and twenty-two and a half games behind Texas. The Mariners basically surrendered any hope of contention in the near future, trading Lee to Texas.

"The truth of the matter is, I lost confidence in Don, Ty, and Rick," the Mariners' general manager, Jack Zduriencik, said. "New leadership is needed and it is needed now. To look around and see so many players having subpar seasons is very disturbing."

Few managers had earned such plaudits, then suffered such

vilification, in the span of just 274 games and a nondescript record of 127-147. Wakamatsu resurfaced the next season as a bench coach for the Toronto Blue Jays, worn down yet considerably calmer.

CECIL COOPER AND THE BUNGLED LINEUP CARD

Several managers have been guilty of questionable lineup decisions or outright mistakes, but they generally knew their starting lineup. Cecil Cooper of the Astros advanced the art form considerably. On May 20, 2009, Cooper decided to significantly juggle his usual batting order, shuffling around four players. He planned to drop the customary leadoff man, Kaz Matsui, into the second slot while promoting Michael Bourn to the leadoff position. Cooper informed these two players about the decision before the game but then filled out his lineup card the usual way—with Matsui leading off and Bourn batting second. On top of that, Cooper posted the lineup late, so the players were less likely to catch the error. "I was waiting to talk to a couple of guys," Cooper said. "That might have created a problem."

Bourn came to the plate first, as the switch was originally intended. Cooper, meanwhile, was thoroughly confused by then and wasn't quite sure which lineup card he had handed in to the plate umpire, Eric Cooper—yes, the ump had the same last name, rendering this account even more befuddling.

Bourn immediately singled to right, and Ken Macha, manager of the Milwaukee Brewers, protested the batting order to the umpire Cooper. Matsui, the second batter, who was supposed to bat first, was called out, and Bourn came to bat for a second straight time to start the game. While it is not terribly unusual for a batting order gaffe to occur after a double switch or in a late inning, nobody could remember the wrong batter coming to the plate to lead off a game.

"We have three or four safeguards, two or three coaches and myself," Cecil Cooper said. "And today no one checked it. So we're all at fault, but I take the blame ultimately because it's my responsibility. That should be the end of it."

Except, of course, it wasn't. First there was the statistical mess to navigate. Matsui was 0 for 1 without batting, while Bourn's single was nullified. The Astros beat the Brewers, yet Cooper never quite shook the image of a first-time manager who wasn't ready for the role. In September, he was replaced by Dave Clark with thirteen games left in the 2009 season, with a record of 70-80 and a seven-game losing streak after getting swept in Milwaukee. Not all the futility was his fault. The club's pitching acquisitions, Russ Ortiz and Mike Hampton, were a disappointment. The Astros two supposed stars, first baseman Lance Berkman and ace Roy Oswalt, both endured subpar seasons. The Astros had last won the National League in 2005, then underperformed for four years, so this was nothing so different. The players felt badly for Cooper, a nice guy. He had been the first black manager in Astros' history and had come highly recommended by Commissioner Bud Selig after Cooper's eleven playing seasons with the Brewers. Ironically, it was the early bungle against Milwaukee, and then the lost series against the Brewers, that doomed his tenure. The players couldn't really argue too vociferously with the dismissal.

"It seems like we've been on a gradual downward spiral," Berkman said. "You can't just point to one thing. I think there are several factors. But if there was an environment for sweeping change or reform, this would be it."

Just like that, another manager was thrown under the bus. Hopefully, the right bus.

BUDDY BELL AND LOSING AS A WAY OF LIFE

Buddy Bell was born into baseball and surely deserved a better send-off. His dad, Gus, played for the Pittsburgh Pirates, and Buddy had a long, fruitful career as a third baseman with Cleveland, Texas, Cincinnati, and Houston. Buddy was a solid hitter, a fabulous glove man. On paper, after an eighteen-year playing career in the majors and then several years as a coach, Bell seemed like a perfect managerial candidate. Instead, he became one of the most consistently unsuccessful managers in the history of baseball.

He took over the Tigers in 1996, then resigned late in the 1998 season because, he said, he "couldn't stand the losing." He'd posted a three-year total of 184-277 in Detroit. Then he managed the Colorado Rockies from 2000 to 2002, when he was fired at the start of that last season with a record of 6-16 and a three-year mark of 161-185. He wasn't finished yet. For some reason, the chronically awful Kansas City Royals hired Bell as their manager in May 2005, inflicting further pain upon him. He proceeded to win his first four games. But in September 2006, he took a medical leave to remove a cancerous growth in his throat. Then in mid-season of 2007—a year that the Royals would finish with a 69-93 record—Bell declared he would soon resign, not long after the Royals finally put together winning records in June and July.

"It doesn't have anything to do with what we've been through in Kansas City," he said when he announced his decision. "I wanted to wait until things got better and then decide if I still felt this way. It started last year when I got sick. My priorities changed real quickly. Not seeing my grandkids became important. When I grew up, my dad wasn't there. When my kids grew up, I wasn't there. Now my grandkids are growing up, and I haven't seen them."

Altogether, Bell's teams in Detroit and Kansas City finished with identical .399 winning percentages under his guidance. Counting his stint in Colorado, Bell's teams were 519-724, or .418. None of these teams placed higher than third in its division. During eight of his nine managerial seasons, Bell's clubs finished in fourth or fifth place—and fifth happened to be last place in the division.

This record of futility cemented Bell's reputation as a competent yet enduring loser. He had been an All-Star five times in his playing career and a Gold Glove winner six times. But Bell set a major-league record of 3,648 games as a player and a manager without ever qualifying for a single playoff game. By comparison, Ernie Banks played 2,528 games for the Cubs without a playoff game (Banks was never rewarded with a managerial gig, because the team's owner, Phil Wrigley, thought he was too nice).

For some reason, none of this sustained failure discouraged Bell's progeny from following in their father's and grandfather's footsteps. Both David and Mike Bell became third basemen in the majors, just like their grandpa Gus and their dad, Buddy, only with somewhat diminished success. But unlike Buddy, David made it to the World Series.

BOTTOM TEN

1   **GENE MAUCH**   So close, and yet so self-destructive.

2   **STUMP MERRILL**   It takes commitment and incompetence to lose in the Bronx.

3   **LEE ELIA**   Don't knock the paying fans, even if they're unemployed.

4   **ROY HARTSFIELD**   During birth of the Blue Jays, he suffered expansion pains.

5   **JIMMY DYKES**   Twenty-one seasons, zero titles. That's consistency.

6   **DON WAKAMATSU**   Went from genius to Captain Queeg in one season.

7   **CECIL COOPER**   Rule of thumb: a manager should know his starting lineup.

8   **BUDDY BELL**   Said he couldn't stand losing, but experienced it 724 times.

9   **WILLIE RANDOLPH**   Smart, nervous manager blew a seven-game lead with seventeen games left for the Mets in 2007.

10   **TED WILLIAMS**   One of the greatest ballplayers in history just kept going downhill with the Senators and Rangers: eighty-six wins in 1969; seventy in 1970; sixty-three in 1971; and fifty-four in 1972.

14 DO AS I SAY, NOT AS I PLAY
The Lousiest Players Turned Geniuses

MANY OF THE most influential figures in baseball—coaches, managers, and general managers—were some of the game's worst players. They might have owned enormous brains, outstanding intuition, wonderful work habits and great social skills, but they simply weren't very good at the sport by major-league standards when they had the chance. Their careers were marked by athletic failure, then professorial success. Considering their miserable playing careers, it is a wonder that anybody hired or heeded them in or around a ballpark.

TOMMY LASORDA, BEFORE HE TOLD PITCHERS HOW TO PITCH

During his twenty-one years as manager of the Los Angeles Dodgers, Tommy Lasorda loved to throw batting practice to his players. He had plenty of practice at it. Lasorda had mostly thrown batting practice to opposing hitters during his three seasons as a lefty reliever and starter from 1954 to 1956 with the Brooklyn Dodgers and the Kansas City A's.

When he was managing, Tommy Lasorda loved to throw batting practice for the Dodgers. Unfortunately, he did a lot of that while he was still a major-league pitcher. *AP Photo*

Pitching in the major leagues was literally Lasorda's dream from childhood. In his autobiography *I Live for This!*, he describes how he would literally dream about pitching for the Yankees. "Then my mother would shake me and say, 'Wake up, Tommy, it's time to go to school!' And I would cry. Why didn't she leave me alone? Why did she wake me from my dream?" But when his fantasies became harsh reality, Lasorda was terrible, posting an ERA of 13.50 during the 1955 season and a 6.48 ERA over his career.

Lasorda was the classic Triple-A talent, a pitcher who consistently excelled at the minor-league level but couldn't get major leaguers out. At five feet, ten inches and with a pudgy face, Lasorda wasn't exactly imposing on the mound. Yet his minor-league exploits were legend. While he was still in the Phillies' farm system with Schenectady in 1948, Lasorda struck out a record twenty-five Amsterdam Rugmakers and banged out the winning RBI single in the fifteenth inning. After fanning fifteen and thirteen batters in his next two outings, he was acquired by the Dodgers in the hopes of developing him as a big-league starter. And with Montreal of the International League in 1953, he was 17-8 with a 2.81 ERA. His pitches didn't translate, however, when Lasorda was promoted the next season.

In one particularly awful relief appearance on May 24, 1955, at Pittsburgh, Lasorda rushed back too soon from injuries and was pounded for four hits, including a homer, and five runs in just two innings during mop-up duty in a 15–1 loss. Two weeks after that meltdown, the Dodgers' general manager, Buzzie Bavasi, called Lasorda into his office and said, "Tommy, we need to cut someone. If you were the general manager on this team, who would you cut?" Lasorda offered an alternative to himself. "If I was in charge, I would cut that Sandy Koufax kid," he said. Koufax was a wild rookie at the time, but Lasorda could tell "that Sandy Koufax kid" had talent and would later admit his recommendation "wasn't about baseball, it was about survival." Bavasi didn't buy it, in any case, returning Lasorda to the minors.

After he was sent back down to Montreal, the scene of many glories, Lasorda became the only player ever to return to a minor-league town after he had been honored with his own day in the ballpark. Lasorda wasn't thrilled to be back there this time, frustrated by his failures with the Dodgers. He acted out, started fights. When the Dodgers released him, Buzzie Bavasi gave him an exit interview and letter that basically told him to stay away permanently. "I was stunned," Lasorda said. "It was like my whole world had collapsed. I didn't know what to do." He begged Bavasi to hire him as a coach, showing him a letter written to Al Campanis, the scouting director, declaring his loyalty to the Dodgers. Bavasi relented and hired him as a scout. "My love for the Dodgers had once again saved my career with the Dodgers," Lasorda said. "And the fun was just beginning."

Lasorda would manage the Dodgers for twenty-one years, winning four pennants and two World Series for teams that amassed records of 1,599-1,439, for a .526 winning percentage, with only six losing seasons in the bunch. He was far better at managing pitchers than he had been at managing pitches.

BILLY BEANE, BEFORE HE WAS BRAD PITT

Billy Beane, Mr. Moneyball, wasn't only a terrible hitter by conventional measurements. The utility outfielder was particularly inept at reaching base—which we all know is Beane's most sacred sabermetric. Beane finished with a career batting average of .219 on four teams from 1984 to 1989 and an on-base percentage of .246. In fact, he only eked out eleven walks altogether in 315 plate appearances and failed to draw even a single base on balls in five of his six seasons. His wins above replacement (WAR) score was –2.1. Beane was a lousy base runner, too, thrown out as often as he was successful stealing. He hit only three homers in 301 at-bats, and the future multimillionaire celebrity/GM never earned a six-figure salary as a player because of these many obvious shortcomings.

To be fair, Beane the GM would never have wasted a high draft pick on Beane the player. As part of his Moneyball philosophy, Beane preferred selecting college-aged and more tested prospects rather than young high school stars. Beane was considered a top prospect as a teenager, a star at virtually every sport he attempted at Mount Carmel High School in California. He was a quarterback on the football team, an ace starting pitcher on the baseball team, and a leading scorer on the basketball team who could dunk with ease at an early age. He learned about baseball from his father, who firmly believed in teaching from how-to manuals. Then with scouts watching closely from the stands during a big high school game, Beane pitched a two-hitter, stole four bases, and ripped three triples. He was drafted in the first round in 1980 by the Mets, who believed he was more polished than their top first-round pick that year, Darryl Strawberry. Beane had dropped to the No. 23 spot in that draft only because he was expected to enroll at Stanford on a scholarship to play quarterback behind John Elway. Instead, Beane signed a $125,000 contract with the Mets, a decision he said was entirely based on money and one he soon regretted. He was assigned to a Class A minor-league team, the Little Falls Mets, where he immediately began to disappoint everyone with a .210 batting average. Even after he was eventually promoted, Beane bounced back and forth to minor-league outposts like Portland, Toledo, and Tacoma.

No matter. Beane's success as a general manager became legend and earned him a fortune. In 2002, he turned down a five-year, $12.5 million offer from the Red Sox to become their general manager. The A's owner, Lew Wolff, made him a partner in the team with 2.5 percent ownership equity, worth about $10 million. As his fame grew through Michael Lewis's book and the ensuing film, Beane's A's unfortunately began to sink in the standings. His reputation as a pioneer, however, was already assured—even if he was not universally respected in all corners of the clubhouse. There is a telling scene in the original screenplay for *Moneyball* in which Beane gives the players a pep talk, while the veteran David Justice bristles at the whole notion.

"I've never seen a GM talk to players," David Justice says.

"You've never seen a GM who was a player," Beane says.

"By player, you mean a guy who couldn't cut it as a player?" asks Justice. "I don't think a guy who couldn't cut it has much to offer guys who can. But go ahead. Tell them how to play baseball. Not me."

Beane tried to distance himself a bit from the movie, explaining to people that some of the script had been fictionalized for Hollywood. In the minds of the general public, though, he is forever Brad Pitt, genial genius. There are worse fates, for a guy with a .246 on-base percentage.

CHARLEY LAU AND HIS FLAWED SWING

Charley Lau, the most celebrated hitting coach in history, was himself a pretty lousy batter. He literally wrote the book on the subject—his *Art of Hitting .300* was published posthumously—yet Lau never managed to reach that mark himself when he had more than twelve at-bats in a season. In eleven years with four teams, Lau amassed a pedestrian .255 average and had several seasons in which his numbers dipped to embarrassing depths. He batted .147 in 1958, .189 in 1960, .194 in 1961, and .189 in 1967. Ironically enough, Lau was living proof during his time in the major leagues that talent cannot always be learned through instruction or theory.

As a defensive catcher, Lau was considered a good game manager without a particularly strong arm. He caught a no-hitter from Warren Spahn but threw out only 28 percent of base stealers during his career. Lau further wrecked his throwing arm toward the end of his career with an overdependence on cortisone shots and a premature return from injuries. At the plate, he demonstrated no great power, hitting only sixteen homers in 1,170 at-bats. His on-base percentage of .318 was no great shakes, either. But then Lau was hired as a batting coach by the Baltimore Orioles, and he developed various theories on the fine art of the swing.

Lau worked hard to improve the mechanics of greater and lesser batters—particularly those with flawed follow-throughs. "I think you could probably swing blindfolded and manage to hit the ball every once in a while," Lau wrote in his book. "The *real* challenge, the thing that can keep ballplayers awake nights, is to hit the ball *consistently*—day after day, in game after game through the season. I wouldn't be surprised if hitting consistently turned out to be the most difficult feat in all sports."

Lau was a big proponent of hitting to all fields and not looking for homers, to avoid the "hero complex." As a player, he
certainly didn't aim for the fences, yet consistency eluded him.
Lau worked with many true believers during his fifteen years
as a hitting coach with the Orioles, A's, Royals, Yankees, and
White Sox. Several stars swore by his instruction. His disciples
included Hal McRae, George Brett, Carlton Fisk, and Greg Luzinski. Some sought out his advice, even if Lau was not coaching
their team. Even after Lau's death, Alex Rodríguez studied Lau's
principles. The coach advocated for a balanced stance, a closed
front foot, and hitting through the swing. He told batters to lose
the tension, to go with the pitch, not decide beforehand to pull
the ball or attempt to go deep.

"After some experimentation and refinement, we came up
with a stance and hitting approach that worked," George Brett
said of his work with Lau. "Little did I realize at the time what it
was going to do and how it was going to change my life. I never
looked back."

Lau's reputation grew so large among baseball insiders that
he was asked to play himself in the 1983 film *Max Dugan Returns*,
hired by the title character to teach a child how to hit for his
Little League games. "Nobody should hit .200," Lau once said.
"Anybody should hit .250." There were several seasons when Lau
himself couldn't manage either feat.

TONY LA RUSSA, GENIUS WITH A DUMB BAT

When Tony La Russa retired in 2011, he went down as one of the
greatest, most innovative managers of all time with six league
championships, three World Series titles, and the third-most
major-league victories with 2,728, behind only Connie Mack
and John McGraw. La Russa was also once a hopelessly over-

matched batter and no better than an average middle infielder
for the Athletics, Braves, and Cubs.

La Russa was drafted in 1962 out of Jefferson High School
in Tampa by the Kansas City Athletics. He signed his first pro
contract on graduation day with great hopes and was called up
to the majors in 1963, at the age of eighteen, after just seventy-six
games in the minors. La Russa made his debut as a pinch runner
on May 10 and was stranded at first base. He was used mostly
as a late-innings pinch runner or defensive replacement, then
finally came to the plate for the first time after fifteen appearances. He was eventually given forty-four at-bats that season,
hitting .250. Everything fell apart during the off-season, when
La Russa hurt his shoulder playing softball with friends.

He spent the next six seasons toiling in the minors before
getting another chance with the Oakland A's in 1968. He would
appear on Opening Day rosters four times, but one occasion in
1968 was his favorite. In Oakland's home opener, in the bottom
of the ninth, La Russa knocked a single on an 0-2 pitch off Dave
McNally of the Orioles. "First pinch hit in Oakland-Alameda
Coliseum history," La Russa proudly said. Still, on May 8, he
received the news he was being demoted. After riding to the
park with Catfish Hunter, he watched the pitcher throw a perfect game against Minnesota from the stands. In July 1970, back
on the roster, La Russa would pop out as a pinch hitter during
Clyde Wright's no-hitter against Oakland.

La Russa became the quintessential journeyman, playing at
different times for farm teams affiliated with the Pirates, the
White Sox, and the Cardinals. In 1973, he appeared in exactly
one game for the Chicago Cubs, his last as a major leaguer. He
was inserted as a pinch runner for Ron Santo on April 6 against
the Expos—the same role he played in his very first game—
and this time successfully scored the winning run in a 3–2 victory, advancing on three successive walks. While he began and
ended his career as a pinch runner, La Russa somehow had zero

stolen bases in his six major-league seasons. He also had no homers in 176 at-bats. Unimpressive at every measurable baseball skill, La Russa was sent back to the minors for four more years. Altogether, he played in 132 major-league games over six seasons, forty times as a starter, with a lifetime batting average just under the Mendoza Line at .199. He had a fairly good eye, walking twenty-three times in 203 total plate appearances. His fielding percentage at second, shortstop, and third base was .960, and he was part of thirty-four double plays.

Along the way, while he was struggling, La Russa made countless important contacts in baseball. On that 1963 team, he traded ideas with his teammates Charlie Lau and Dick Howser. In the minors and then on the A's, La Russa played with the catcher Dave Duncan, who would become his longtime pitching coach. By 1977, when he batted .188 for the New Orleans Pelicans of the American Association, La Russa had seen the writing on the wall and was on his way to earning a law degree from Florida State's College of Law. He would be admitted to the Florida Bar two years later, but by then he had decided to take a post managing in the minor leagues. "I'd rather ride the buses in the minor leagues than practice law for a living," he said. The master showman Bill Veeck eventually gave La Russa his first shot at managing in the big leagues, and the next thirty-three years became history that had little to do with a .199 average.

SPARKY ANDERSON, BEFORE HE HAD SPARK

George Lee Anderson was born the son of a country house painter in Bridgewater, South Dakota. He might have taken up his dad's line of work, but the family moved to Los Angeles when he was eight years old, and George was soon selected as the batboy for the University of Southern California baseball team. He was an infielder for Dorsey High School, then was signed by the Brooklyn Dodgers before the 1953 season. Anderson spent the next six seasons in the minor leagues, earning little except a new nickname, Sparky, from a Fort Worth, Texas, radio announcer. Anderson had a fiery, upbeat temperament. He was a walking, talking pep talk, and most teammates took to him quickly. In December 1958, Anderson was traded by the Los Angeles Dodgers to the Phillies for three players. Considering his minor-league stats at the time, this was a considerable rip-off by the Dodgers, who acquired the modestly successful Rip Repulski in the deal. The Phillies then gave Anderson a real shot at winning the second base job. He played in 152 games that 1959 season, starting most of them.

Unfortunately, Anderson proved downright awful at everything. After a relatively decent start, in which he recorded at least one hit in six of his first seven games, he sank like a rock to a .205 average by the end of May. He finished the season at .218 with no homers for the last-place Phillies. He had a .249 slugging average. He was caught stealing in nine of fifteen attempts. His glove and range at second were below average. His wins above replacement (WAR) was –1.4, meaning the Phils would likely have won one or two more games if they had replaced him with an average second baseman. Not that it would have helped much, considering the last-place Phils, 64-90, finished twenty-three games behind the Dodgers and seven games behind the seventh-place Cardinals.

So it was back to the minors for Anderson, where he labored for four years with the Triple-A Toronto Maple Leafs of the International League, never reaching the .260 batting mark. His stats were truly miserable, yet Anderson never lost heart on the field, and his unrealistic can-do attitude caught the eye of the Maple Leafs' owner, Jack Kent Cooke. In 1964, when Anderson was still only thirty, Cooke offered him the managerial job in Toronto. Anderson gratefully grabbed the post and retired from playing. What followed was an uncanny string of successes managing several minor-league teams. From 1965 through 1968, Anderson's farm teams won four successive pennants in four different minor leagues. He was hired as a third base coach by the Padres in 1969, then was the surprise hire as manager of the Reds in 1970. His minor-league association with the Reds' general manager, Bob Howsam, was the key to this opportunity, and Anderson made the most of it. The Reds would win 102 games and the National League pennant in 1970. Anderson would go on to capture three World Series championships with Cincinnati and Detroit, becoming the first manager to win a title for teams in different leagues. He finished with a managerial record of 2,194-1,834 and was elected to the Hall of Fame by the Veterans Committee in 2000, ten years before his death.

As a rule, Sparky didn't like talking about his flawed playing career, just as he didn't particularly enjoy reminiscing about his successes as manager. "People who live in the past generally are afraid to compete in the present," he said. "I've got my faults, but living in the past is not one of them. There's no future in it."

BOTTOM TEN

1   **TOMMY LASORDA**   He couldn't pitch until he pitched Dodger blue.

2   **BILLY BEANE**   Failed phenom wouldn't have signed himself.

3   **CHARLEY LAU**   Missed on too many swings, no matter how perfect the follow-through.

4   **JOE McCARTHY**   Won seven titles and 1,460 games managing the Yankees, after being stuck in the minors for fifteen years as a second baseman from 1907 to 1921.

5   **TONY LA RUSSA**   Couldn't even reach the Mendoza Line.

6   **SPARKY ANDERSON**   Terrible player on awful Phillies.

7   **WALT ALSTON**   Thirteen years playing infield in the minors and never even made it to Class AAA. Then managed the Dodgers for twenty-three years, with seven National League pennants and four Series titles.

8   **RALPH HOUK**   Managed Mickey Mantle and Roger Maris to two championships after catching in the minors for eight seasons.

9   **JIM LEYLAND**   The career .222 hitter in the minors once said it wasn't the dark, small-stadium conditions that ruined his average. "I could have been inside the Duquesne Light Company, it wouldn't have made a difference." He later won a championship in Florida and a pennant in Detroit.

10   **BILL CARRIGAN**   Platoon catcher hit grand total of six homers in ten years with Boston, then led the Red Sox as manager to successive World Series titles in 1915 and 1916.

15 | BEYOND THE BOSS
The Worst Owners of All Time

FOR MAJOR LEAGUE Baseball teams, winning starts at the top. So does losing and wholesale chaos. There are owners who buy teams for the glory, for the profits, or just because they need the capital depreciation on their tax returns. There are owners who inherit a ball club the way they might inherit a diamond necklace, not really knowing what to do with it. The best ones are bright executives who hire the right people and get out of the way, investing reasonably in the farm system and the forty-man roster. The worst ones dump payroll, blackmail cities into building stadiums, and stick their noses where they definitely don't belong.

Considering that most franchises are now worth a billion dollars or so, it would be nice to think that owners through the decades were responsible for this success story by behaving like reasonable businessmen and businesswomen. That hasn't always been the case.

You won't find George Steinbrenner in this chapter, it should be noted, despite his suspensions, his bullying, his ego, and his outsized economics. That's because the Yankees won seven World Series during his tenure as owner, and every fan in the Bronx willingly endured all that nonsense for all that success.

Those banners flapping on the flagpole make an illegal campaign contribution to Richard Nixon appear very trivial indeed.

HORACE FOGEL AND HIS VERY BAD IDEAS

Long before Horace Fogel was banned for life from baseball, the future owner came up with one of the dumbest notions in the sport's history. Fogel was managing the New York Giants in 1902—for reasons few understood, even at the time—when he suddenly came to the conclusion that Christy Mathewson should be converted from pitcher to a field position. This was quite some time before Babe Ruth was shifted from pitcher to the outfield, so you have to give Fogel credit for ingenuity, if nothing else. But in 1902, Mathewson, still only twenty-one, was coming off a twenty-win season with a 2.41 ERA. Fogel thought Mathewson was overrated as a pitching prospect, that he was too wild, and auditioned him in the outfield and at first base—where Mathewson committed four errors in three games. This experiment was considered absolute folly by the New York reporters covering the team and by Mathewson's teammates, who all knew better. Fogel also openly criticized his players in the newspapers, and soon there was a mutiny of sorts. He was fired from the Giants after only two months with an 18-23 mark, while Mathewson went on to win 373 games in his career with a 2.13 career ERA. Meanwhile, Mathewson finished with a batting average of .215 and only seven homers in 1,687 at-bats, further proving Fogel's belief to be utterly wrongheaded.

Fogel was an exceptionally colorful personality, a chronic conspiracy theorist who earned his pay at times as a sportswriter. He wrote columns for *The Philadelphia Press* in early 1883 before taking a job as the official scorekeeper for the Athletics. Within four years, through connections, he was hired as manager of the Indianapolis Hoosiers of the National League. The Hoosiers, on

their way to a last-place finish, were 20-49 under Fogel before he
was dumped. He then returned to writing, becoming associate
editor of *Sporting Life*. Fogel kept at this for about fifteen years,
before he was offered the manager's post with the Giants in 1902,
leading to the Mathewson fiasco.

Back he went again to sportswriting, this time for the Philadelphia *Telegraph*. Journalistically speaking, Fogel was known
as a reactionary, gushing with praise for teams on win streaks
and ripping them when they lost. He had a high public profile, if nothing else, and became the front man for an ownership group that purchased the Phillies in November 1909 for a
price approaching $500,000. That group, according to research
by PhillySports.com, reportedly included Charles Murphy, who
was also president of the Chicago Cubs, raising many eyebrows
but never quite spurring an official probe.

With the Phillies, Fogel had real power and a large platform
for his impractical notions. He changed the team's uniforms,
which suddenly sported a large Old English *P* and green-striped
socks. Then he decided to change the team name, announcing
that *Phillies* "has come to mean a comfortable lackadaisicalness,
the fourth-place groove." When the name Quakers was suggested, Fogel bristled. "Quakers stands for peaceful people who
will dodge a fight. We're not going to be that way. We're going
to get into fights."

Fogel decided his team would be called the Philadelphia Live
Wires. His new logo featured an eagle grasping some crackling
electric wires. This was a time, however, before broadcasters
quickly bought into every stadium and club name change. Fans
and newspapers resisted. The team nickname remained the
Phillies.

Fogel was Bill Veeck before there was a Bill Veeck. Pigeons
would fly from his ballpark, distributing free tickets to games.
He once arranged for a wedding on the field, with a lion serving
as witness to the marriage. There were concerts and circuses

and all kinds of entertainment that he hoped would keep spectators' minds off the Phils' continued fourth- and fifth-place finishes. Fogel finally got himself into real trouble in 1912, when he told some old reporter friends, over drinks, that National League officials were conspiring to hand the Giants the pennant over the Cubs. He kept it up, too. Fogel complained that the Cardinals' manager, Roger Bresnahan, wasn't fielding his best lineup against the Giants. Then he sent a fateful, foolish letter to Thomas Lynch, in which he accused the league president of ordering umpires to make calls for the Giants in games against the Phillies. He contended in one Chicago newspaper interview that the Giants were handed at least twenty-one victories by unfair umpiring, and Fogel continued a self-destructive letter-writing campaign to his fellow owners. Finally, Lynch could take no more. The National League president wrote:

As far as President Fogel's attacks on the President of the National League is concerned, I care nothing. My twenty-five years' record in baseball speaks for itself. The cowardly attack on the honesty of the umpires and the game itself is a different matter, however, and cannot be overlooked. . . . Regardless of whether Mr. Fogel has a financial interest in the Philadelphia Club or not, he is the president of that organization, and the charges he makes can only be handled by the league itself.

There was a brief investigation of the alleged conspiracy, which found no supporting evidence. After a hearing in New York on November 27, 1912, Fogel resigned as president of the Phillies in the hope that would suffice. Instead, by a 7–0 vote of the other owners, Fogel was found guilty of damaging the integrity of baseball and was banned from baseball for life. He continued muckraking, reporting in 1920 in *The Philadelphia Inquirer* that the 1905 and 1908 World Series had been fixed. By then, Fogel had cried wolf several times too often, and nobody paid much attention to the man who once thought Mathewson was a natural first baseman.

MARGE SCHOTT, NUTTY LADY

When the automobile magnate Charles Schott died in 1968 of a heart attack in his mistress's bathtub, his chain-smoking widow, Marge, suddenly inherited a ton of money. This eventually became very bad news for the Cincinnati Reds, because in 1984 Schott decided to invest $11 million for controlling interest in her favorite baseball club and, in her own words, "save the team for Cincinnati."

Schott was the daughter of a local German-American lumber businessman, Edward Unnewehr, who had instilled in her his prejudices but not his discipline. "My father was Achtung-German," she once said. "He used to ring a bell when he wanted my mother." During her fifteen-year reign of destructive weirdness at the helm of the Reds, from 1984 to 1999, the club enjoyed what amounted to average success on the field. They made the playoffs only twice, though they did win a World Series in 1990 under their manager, Lou Piniella. But the public relations damage she perpetrated was irreparable. There wasn't an ethnic or minority group she didn't offend, and Schott tortured her own players and managers with eccentric demands that included rubbing them with the fur of her dog (Schottzie or Schottzie 02) or simply sending them the fur in envelopes. She would order top club executives to walk these dogs on the field and then interrogate them, "Tinkle or poo?"

"I'd have quite a bit of dog hair," recalled Jack McKeon, her last manager. "I was hoping we didn't lose too many games because she would always come down."

Unfortunately, Schott's eccentricities were not limited to such

Who names her dog after herself? Marge Schott, that's who.
Here she drags poor, ever-present Schottzie onto *Late Night
with David Letterman*. *AP Photo/Ray Stubblebine*

quaint, innocuous acts. She was famously cheap and racist. She
destroyed the team's farm system because it was costing too
much. She tried not to pay players on the disabled list, complaining once that José Rijo was costing her "three million dollars to
sit on his butt." She cut off the out-of-town scores on the outfield board in order to save the $350 subscription price, and she
turned off the computers in the Reds' offices to save electricity.

Her craziness escalated substantially in the 1990s, while she
was going through five managers in six years. A former marketing director for the Reds, Cal Levy, testified in a court deposition
that he heard Schott call Eric Davis and Dave Parker "million-
dollar niggers." Her record on hiring blacks in the organization
was terrible. An Oakland A's official, Sharon Jones, was quoted
by *The New York Times* as saying that she heard Schott say before
an owners' conference call, "I would never hire another nigger.
I'd rather have a trained monkey."

During this time, it was also revealed that Schott displayed a Nazi swastika armband in her home. She did not deny this, though she insisted the armband was a gift of appreciation given to her husband by an American soldier for saving his life. A few years later, unfortunately, she went on to say Hitler "was good in the beginning" for Germany but "went too far." She said in her own court deposition that she was not prejudiced against Jews. "They are not smarter than us, just sharper," she said.

In a speech before the Ohio County Treasurers Association in May 1994, Schott said her players were not permitted to wear earrings because "only fruits wear earrings." She was also cited in *Sports Illustrated* for putting on a thick Japanese accent while mimicking the prime minister of Japan. For all this nonsense, Schott was fined $250,000 and suspended from day-to-day operations of the Reds during the 1993 season, then suspended again in 1996. Schott learned nothing from it. She was completely unrepentant when she sold a controlling interest in the club for $67 million in 1999 and right up to her death at age seventy-five in 2004.

"I don't know what I would have done differently, except for stood up and fought with the boys a little more," she said after selling the Reds—who finished twenty-five games out of first place in her final season.

Schott kept down the price of tickets and hot dogs in Cincinnati. She also set back by several decades the image of women sports executives in America.

FRANK McCOURT AND THE VERY EXPENSIVE DIVORCE

Frank McCourt met his wife, Jamie, when they were freshmen at Georgetown University in the early 1970s, a long way from Los Angeles. Alas, this encounter would come back to haunt the proud Dodgers franchise some forty years later, when the couple's very public divorce demolished the moral and financial underpinnings of the team once run by the dignified Branch Rickey.

McCourt, a parking lot mogul in Boston, first tried to purchase—and in all likelihood wreck—his hometown Red Sox. He planned to tear down Fenway Park and build a new stadium in its place. Fortunately for the Sox, that team was sold to an ownership group led by John Henry in 2002. McCourt then set his sights on the Dodgers, purchasing the club for $430 million from Rupert Murdoch's News Corp. The financing of this deal was something of a house of cards and probably should have been rejected outright by Commissioner

The McCourts—emphasis on "Court"—during pre-divorce times, when ex-Dodgers owners Frank and Jamie were still on smiling terms. *AP Photo/Carlos Delgado*

Bud Selig and other owners. McCourt used his South Boston parking lot as collateral for the debt-driven agreement.

The owner hired as general manager Paul DePodesta, the Moneyball genius who was not such an insightful guru with the Dodgers. Some bad deals were done, but generally all was copacetic until October 2009—when Frank and Jamie went public with their separation while the Dodgers were still involved in the playoffs. One day after the Dodgers lost to the Phils in the National League Championship Series, Jamie was fired from her job as CEO of the ball club and soon filed for one of the messiest and costliest divorces in California's acrimonious legal history. Frank accused her of having an affair with a chauffeur while insisting the Dodgers would be kept out of all conflicts. "My personal situation and divorce has no bearing on the team whatsoever," McCourt said. "I own the team and we're moving forward as we have in the past six years. We're committed to developing young players, more so than ever. We've invested heavily in that area. And we're in the trade and free-agent markets to see if we can improve the team."

That never happened. The Dodgers' player payroll shrank from $120 million in 2008 to $100 million in 2009 and then to $95 million in 2010. The team was no longer bidding for top free agents. In December 2010, a judge invalidated a postnuptial agreement that would have protected Frank McCourt's ownership of the franchise from his wife. The two exes remained dysfunctional co-owners until October 2011, when Jamie gave up her share of the Dodgers for $130 million. By then, McCourt was desperately trying to wring dollars out of every conceivable resource. He signed a twenty-year broadcasting rights deal with Fox for a reported $3 billion that was quickly nixed by Major League Baseball. He also received a personal loan from Fox to meet payroll, promising to pay the money back from the settlement he hoped to gain against yet another law firm. There were also reports of IRS investigations into the McCourts' operation of the Dodgers and a separate probe of the club's charitable foundation.

Commissioner Bud Selig finally took action, appointing an overseer for the team, Tom Schieffer, hoping to force a sale. "The Dodgers have been one of the most prestigious franchises in all of sports," Selig said. "We owe it to their legion of loyal fans to ensure that this club is being operated properly now and will be guided appropriately in the future." McCourt bristled and wouldn't budge, claiming he was in compliance with all guidelines. "It is hard to understand the commissioner's action," McCourt said.

Eventually, the Dodgers filed for bankruptcy under Chapter 11, and McCourt agreed to sell the team. "It's been a privilege to own this franchise," he said. "My focus is to make sure that I hand it off in better shape than I found it." He sold it for $2.15 billion to a group including Magic Johnson, making a tidy profit to cover his debts. By that measure, and only that measure, McCourt was a great success.

THE WILPONS AND MR. MADOFF

It is hard to argue with the numbers, which suggest that Fred and Jeff Wilpon inflicted considerable suffering upon the New York Mets both on and off the diamond. The club lost $120 million in just two seasons, 2010 and 2011, despite a new ballpark and leading to an all-time record for cutting payroll in a single off-season. Meanwhile, the Mets went from contention in 2008 to several successive seasons in which they failed to reach eighty victories, finishing out of first each year by at least eighteen games.

A big part of this story was the Wilpons' involvement with the swindler Bernie Madoff. They invested about $1.6 billion in Madoff's pyramid scheme, walked off with hundreds of millions of dollars in profits, and then found themselves in an extended, expensive legal war fending off Irving Picard, a trustee representing the victims of the fraud. The Wilpons had recommended Madoff's investment firm to friends while claiming complete ignorance of—not, as was charged by Madoff's victims, "willful blindness" to—the con man's deception.

Instead of cracking down on this ownership team as he had done with Frank McCourt, Bud Selig became an enabler of the Wilpons, his longtime friends. Major League Baseball extended a $25 million loan to aid ownership, without assuming control over operations of the franchise. The Wilpons borrowed another $40 million from Bank of America. The father and son then began attempting to sell off pieces of the team as if they were shares in a barren oil field.

Most owners would agree to yield control upon reaching

Fred and Jeff Wilpon celebrate the birth of Citi Field,
before the Bernie Madoff scandal turned everything desperate
for the Mets owners. *AP Photo/Ed Betz*

such a crisis, but the Wilpons held on to the Mets for dear life.
Fred retained a deep, romantic link to baseball past and to the
Brooklyn Dodgers. He was a teammate of Sandy Koufax's on the
Lafayette High School baseball team in Brooklyn and a longtime
admirer of Jackie Robinson. The Wilpons were accused at times
in New York of being more appreciative of the Dodgers' history
than the Mets' own tradition—particularly when they built a
Jackie Robinson rotunda at their new Citi Field without, at first,
a Hall of Fame to honor past Mets stars like Tom Seaver. Despite
all these controversies, the Wilpons would not budge.

"[The fans] shouldn't be concerned about us owning the franchise," Fred Wilpon said before the 2012 season. "We intend to
own the franchise for a very long time. Whether they're happy
about that right now, I don't know." The fans weren't happy at
all, of course. Eventually, in March 2012, the Wilpons settled the

lawsuit with Picard for $162 million. They paid back their loans, too, but faced years of budget tightening.

Fred Wilpon first bought a 1 percent stake in the Mets in 1980, then a 50 percent share in 1986, before assuming full control of the club in 2002. His son, Jeff, began making the biggest decisions, which included the clumsy firing of Willie Randolph during a West Coast road trip. Slowly, the Mets fell from contention to third-rate status in the National League East. During and after the 2011 season, they lost their two biggest stars, José Reyes and Carlos Beltrán, largely because they could no longer afford them. This was hardly the way to compete with their interborough rivals, the Yankees. Scott Boras, the super-agent, urged the Wilpons to sell. He said the club "used to shop in the steaks aisle and now they're in the fruits and nuts section." The Wilpons were entrenched, however, and going nowhere. They could not be traded or released, to the great regret of Mets fans.

CHARLIE FINLEY, ALL-AROUNDER

Charlie Finley covered all the bases, becoming a pioneer for modern-day owners who would follow. He disassembled a championship team, long before Jeffrey Loria did the same thing to the Florida Marlins. He was incredibly cheap, before David Glass in Kansas City and Robert Nutting in Pittsburgh turned small-market stinginess into an art form. Finley meddled in baseball operations in often foolish ways, much the way Peter Angelos would interfere in Baltimore. And Finley moved his franchise out of one city and teased several other municipalities, a common tactic of today's owners in search of the best deal.

There are really two tales of Charlie Oscar Finley: one before the age of free agency, when his methods were still viable and proved remarkably successful; and one after free agency, when he could not, or would not, compete. Finley was a glorified insurance agent from Indiana when he first bought controlling interest in the Kansas City Athletics on December 19, 1960, paying $1.975 million to the widow of Arnold Johnson for 52 percent of the team. He had an obsessive dislike of the New York Yankees, and at first this inspiration served him well. He cut off all

Charlie Finley and Charlie O.; Charlie Finley is the
one on top. *AP Photo/William Straeter*

deals with the Yanks, who had used the Athletics as something of a farm team for many years, most famously in the acquisition of the young slugger Roger Maris a year earlier. He ordered his public address announcer to declare that balls hit past a certain line in right field would have been homers into the short right-field porch at Yankee Stadium. He also invested money in the team's minor-league system, which paid enormous dividends.

Finley became deeply involved in every aspect of his losing team, including marketing. He changed the club's uniform colors in 1963 to gold, green, and white, then their cleats from black to white in 1967. Mickey Mantle took one look at these New Wave outfits and sneered, "They should have come out of the dugout on tippy-toes, holding hands and singing." Finley phased out the name Athletics, replacing it with A's. He introduced a new mascot, Charlie O. the mule, who had free rein over the entire stadium. He installed a mechanical rabbit to pop out near home plate and deliver fresh baseballs to the umpires. He tried out orange baseballs during exhibition games and offered players bonuses for growing mustaches. He championed the designated hitter, before its time. None of this was particularly harmful. But he played nasty politics with Kansas City, often threatening to move the club. He signed a new four-year lease with Municipal Stadium, then filed a lawsuit, hoping to rescind the agreement. He tried to relocate the A's to Louisville, but the owners vetoed the agreement. Finally, in 1965, the American League's president, Joe Cronin, fashioned a compromise allowing Finley to move the A's within three years. Those lame-duck seasons in Kansas City were ugly in every way and included a player mutiny led by Ken Harrelson and supported by the manager, Alvin Dark, who was fired.

Finley brought the franchise to the Oakland Coliseum in 1968, just as the club was emerging as a dynasty behind Reggie Jackson, Catfish Hunter, Vida Blue, Joe Rudi, Sal Bando, and Rollie Fingers. The A's won three straight World Series from 1972 to 1974, a feat not repeated until the Yankees managed the same run from 1998 to 2000. Such success only made Finley more restless. He became furious his champion A's weren't drawing bigger crowds in Oakland and began flirting with another move to Seattle, Denver, or Toronto. During the 1974 World Series, Finley went on a national television broadcast to declare that the city of Oakland could not support Major League Baseball. He grew cheaper than ever, charging players for their broken bats and cutting back on his famous promotions.

The advent of free agency became Finley's true undoing. He lost Catfish Hunter to the Yankees after a lengthy legal fight over a contractual technicality, then peddled his best players like spare parts. He traded Jackson to Baltimore. Finley negotiated deals totaling $3.5 million, selling Blue to the Yankees and Fingers and Rudi to Boston, but Commissioner Bowie Kuhn vetoed the transactions "in the best interests of baseball." Finley called Kuhn "the village idiot" and kept hawking his players. Most of his stars simply left via free agency. He fought desperately, to no avail, against the concept of salary arbitration. "We'll be the nation's biggest assholes if we do this," Finley said when owners agreed to the arbitration process in 1973. "You can't win. You'll have guys with no baseball background setting salaries. You'll have a system that drives up the average salary every year. Give them anything they want, but don't give them arbitration."

By 1979, when the A's went 54-108, attendance in Oakland was a pathetic 306,763. After trying again but failing to shift the A's to either Denver or New Orleans, Finley finally gave up the hunt in August 1980 and sold the club for $12.7 million to the Haas family, owners of Levi Strauss. Finley lost much of those profits over the next years on bad business deals before dying of heart disease on February 19, 1996, at age seventy-seven.

"I think Charlie will be remembered probably as a maverick," Kuhn said after Finley's death. "Charlie was Charlie. He didn't like people telling him what to do. He liked to do his thing, his own way."

BOTTOM TEN

1	**HORACE FOGEL**	Banned from baseball, about ten years too late.
2	**MARGE SCHOTT**	Swastikas, dog fur, and racist slurs. Enough said.
3	**HARRY FRAZEE**	Red Sox owner from 1916 to 1923, who drove the proud franchise into the ground and sold Babe Ruth to the Yankees.
4	**FRANK McCOURT**	Dodgers fans are relieved he finally divorced them.
5	**THE WILPONS**	Harder to shake than nits from a full head of hair.
6	**CHARLIE FINLEY**	So many ideas, so little time.
7	**CALVIN GRIFFITH**	Cheapskate owner moved the Senators to Minnesota in 1961 because, he said, "I found out you only had 15,000 blacks [in Minneapolis]. Black people don't go to ballgames. . . . You've got good, hardworking white people here."
8	**WILLIAM COX**	Bought the Phils in 1943 and started working out with the team since he'd played baseball at Yale. His players mutinied by mid-season. He made "sentimental bets" on the Phillies and was suspended.
9	**PETER ANGELOS**	Purchased the Orioles in 1993, threw money at the wrong players, and dissipated all good feelings at Camden Yards.
10	**JEFFREY LORIA**	Doomed the Expos in Montreal, then sold the 2003 championship Marlins team for parts.